No Face Like Mine

Martha Wyatt-Rossignol

Copyright © 2024 Martha Wyatt-Rossignol
All rights reserved
First Edition

PAGE PUBLISHING
Conneaut Lake, PA

First originally published by Page Publishing 2024

ISBN 979-8-89315-629-4 (hc)
ISBN 979-8-89157-150-1 (digital)

Printed in the United States of America

Preface

This book is dedicated to my late sisters, Dorothy "Dot" Wyatt-Robinson and Ruth Ann Wyatt. Ruth, I wish you were here to read this because I know you would be proud of me. Dot, you were just like a mother to me; I know you would be proud as well.

After hearing about some of a good friend's childhood experiences, I was inspired to write about her story. People in similar situations should read this powerful story and know they are not alone in this world. I want to thank everyone who helped me along the way, especially my dear friend for sharing her life with me. Thank you, Sonya Lee, for giving me so many wonderful ideas to effectively tell this story. Thank you, Velma Kaye Oliver, my creative niece, for designing my book cover. The abstract face with no identity truly represents quite well the passages between the book cover. The broken image with its vast array of colors depicts a woman in turmoil with no clear indication of who she truly is. Lastly, I want to thank my family and friends for their continued encouragement and support. Without you, none of this would have been possible.

Note this story is fictional to protect the privacy of certain individuals. The names and identifying details have been changed.

Chapter 1

Most days blur together, but there are some that stand out more than others. Those are the ones that seem to have the ability to change the course of your life for the good and sometimes for the bad. I'll never forget one particular good day. It all began at the Bermuda Airport back in 2003.

We both were there for the same purpose: to pick up a family member. I was picking up my niece who was coming for a visit, and she was picking up her daughter, who was also coming for a visit. The heat was unbearable that day, and the humidity made it feel worse. While I was standing outside trying to fan the heat away with my bare hands, this sort of short, slightly medium-built lady with beautifully shaped legs walked up to me and asked, "Excuse me, ma'am, do you know if we have to pay for parking?" She was wearing a lavender blouse with a pair of tan cargo shorts.

Startled, I replied, "I don't think so," looking around.

She quickly said with a smile, "I didn't mean to startle you." I did notice she had a pleasant smile.

I replied, "I'm not sure, but I parked my car right over there," with a wave of my hand. I hadn't really thought about it. I didn't see any parking meters when I drove up, so I just parked my car without thinking about paying.

Then I said, "Although there's nothing free in Bermuda, but now that you mentioned it, I didn't see any meters when I drove in." She nodded knowingly, the way another Bermuda resident would.

Then she said, "I just wanna make sure," her hazel eyes shirking from the hot rays of the sun. "Don't need no surprises coming up out of here." As we looked around, however, we realized the parking lot was under construction, and the pay and park meters had been removed.

"Well, what do you know?" I said. "I guess we don't have to pay for parking today because there are no meters." We both shared a good, hardy laugh about that one.

The minute we become aware of each other's American accents, we struck up a conversation, almost immediately talking as if we had known each other all our lives. She was very easy to talk to, which made me feel very comfortable with her. We talked about our children, our connection to Bermuda, and our husbands, all in that short span while waiting for a plane to land. "Where are you from originally?" I asked.

"Jasper, Missouri," she said. "And you?"

I said, "A small town in Mississippi." I didn't give the name because the town is so small most had never even heard of it.

Suddenly, we heard music playing inside the terminal coming from the Calypso Band, which meant the people had deplaned and had started coming into the airport. The music was a form of welcoming the tourists to the island while also welcoming the locals back home. We knew then it wouldn't be long before people would be filing out of the airport looking for rides, whether it be a relative, a friend, or a taxi. Those people that were looking for taxis exited to the left, and the ones that were being picked up by a friend or a relative exited to the right. There were about fifteen taxis already waiting in line to pick up passengers as they made their way out of the airport to take them to their destination. Some taxi drivers suddenly got out of their car holding cardboard signs with names on them. Most times, those were people coming in for business. We quickly exchanged phone numbers as we were stretching our necks looking through the crowds for our loved ones.

I finally saw my niece waving as she made her way through the crowd. We picked up our respective family members and parted ways with promises to stay in touch with little realization at the time that this was the beginning of a lifelong friendship.

No Face Like Mine

I often thought about the lady I met the at airport over the next several weeks; I just couldn't get her off my mind. She was definitely someone I wanted to get to know. I made a mental note to contact her after my niece's visit was over. Since I'm a person who always tries to make good on promises, a month or so later, I called her up and invited her and her husband over for dinner.

Our husbands got to meet each other, and the four of us hit it off, so much so that she and I started hanging out together. Gee (that's her name) and I would often get together while our husbands were at work on Saturdays and make our traditional American meals—grilled chicken, potato salad, mustard greens, etc.—eating and enjoying each other's company, talking about the good old days. We went to the beach occasionally to dip our feet in the beautiful blue water and to take a stroll on the sparkling pink sand. Neither of us could swim, but it was always nice to be at the beach lazing in the sun watching other swimmers or just people-watching while other water sports were being performed. It was always fun to see families and friends there gathered with their children, eating picnic lunches and building sand castles and such. We became a constant in each other's lives.

Gee often talked a lot about her family. During our conversations, she always commented that her mother was a little crazy, which I thought was odd and a very unusual way to describe one's mother. She said that whenever her mother called her, she didn't answer the phone immediately or even on the same day. She had to wait a day or two before calling her back because she had to be in a certain mood to have a conversation with her. "Now that I think about it, I don't really have to talk to her at all," she told me. "She does all the talking. All I have to do is listen with a response every now and again." She laughed and shook her head. "When I'm working, most times, I just lay the phone down on my desk with the speaker on and continue doing what I'm doing."

When she noticed the frown on my face, she chuckled and said, "Girl, you just have to meet my mother to understand her, and then you would understand what I'm talking about."

Again, I thought that was a very strange way to describe one's mother, but I just shrugged and said to myself, *I guess she would know better than I.*

I always listened intently to her views on each of her family members when she talked about them and found myself trying to visualize the faces of each relative as she spoke of them. Her family seemed so different from my fairly conventional one. They seemed like a colorful cast of characters full of mystery. She said her mother had five siblings, Mattie and Pattie (the twins), Cida, Harry, and Jimmy. When she mentioned Cida, I wondered where in the world that name came from. I thought it was short for something else, but I later found out that was the actual name Gee's grandmother had given her. I got to meet three of the siblings out of the five. She did say Pattie, her mother, and Mattie were identical twins. Whereas most twins seem to have a stronger bond for each other than mere siblings, these two, according to Gee, shared an animosity that was very blatant. Apparently, it was so strong one could feel the dislike they had for each other. After meeting them, I must admit, Gee's mother intrigued me the most.

Cida, the oldest, when I met her, seemed very reserved with a twinkle in her eyes but also full of mystery. I couldn't help but think, after I had met the three sisters, that these sisters had closets of secrets so deep that it would take years to get through them. Later, I would find out that their secrets were so heavy and deep that they permeated throughout the entire family. I didn't meet the brothers in the family, just the three girls. The characters Gee described when talking about her family were unforgettable. Her descriptions of them were always so vivid, which embedded them in my memory. I thought about the members of her family often, especially Pattie and Mattie. I had a feeling that those two carried a deeper, darker secret, and I believe they knew what each other's secret was. It was just a gut feeling I had after meeting them and talking with them.

In 2014, the two of us decided it was time to introduce each other to our respective families. We had known each other eleven years by then. We made reservations to fly to Georgia, where she had a house, stay there for a few days, and then make our plans. We decided to drive to Clareville, Mississippi, where I was from, to meet my family first.

We spent three days at Gee's house preparing and mapping out our plans for our road trip. On that fourth day, we got up around four o'clock in the morning to get an early start. We packed the car and started our journey. It was going to be about an eight-hour drive from her house to my hometown, so an early start was a necessity. We talked about everything and anything all the way there, which made the trip seem to go by faster. We had packed the car with goodies and snacks so we wouldn't have to do much stopping along the way.

As we neared my hometown, I said, "Gee, let's drive down Main Street, and you can have a quick peek at the little town that I called home for many years." I could clearly see the changes as we cruised through. It was a very windy day, and debris was flying everywhere. Clareville is usually very hot and humid, but today, the strong winds made it a little more bearable. I stretched my neck looking as we were driving through, trying to see if I saw anyone that I recognized standing or just milling around on the streets. I finally gave up and gave Gee directions as to how to get to my sister's house where we would be staying, telling her that we would tour the town later. We needed to get out the car to rest and stretch our legs.

We were going to stay with my sister Ann. When we arrived at Ann's house, two of my sisters were already there waiting to welcome us. They were sitting on the porch sipping sweet ice tea. Sweet tea is a big thing in the South. I introduced Gee to my sisters, my nieces and nephews, cousins, and some of my childhood friends. Ann's house was packed with family and friends. Somehow, someone had wedged a card table into a corner, and some of my nieces and nephews were playing a card game. Of course, there was lots of food on the table waiting for us, and after the introductions and some small talk, we gathered in the kitchen to eat the meal Ann had prepared. The aroma of the food was overwhelming. Everything looked delicious. Ann had prepared all my favorites—red beans and rice, stuffed cabbage, baked chicken, fried pork chops, fried okra, and of course, corn bread. "I couldn't let you come and not have your favorite meal cooked," Ann said laughing.

I looked around and saw what she had prepared for dessert. "Oh my, we have German chocolate cake! I haven't had that in a long time," I said. We stuffed ourselves as we talked and caught up with what had been going on since we'd last seen each other.

Gee was in awe of my family and their warmth. I could tell because she kept saying how wonderful everyone was to her. She said, "Girl, you have a beautiful family. They are treating me like they have known me all of their lives, and they make me feel so welcome."

Two days later, we toured my small town, which wasn't much to see anymore. A lot had changed since I left. I guess the biggest change for me was seeing how rundown and dilapidated the town had become. The main street now had boarded-up windows on what used to be thriving businesses. Some buildings had Closed signs hanging on them, and they looked as if they had been closed for years. The few businesses that were still open now had iron bars on both the doors and windows. The town I had grown up in had little resemblance to the town I was now seeing. There was graffiti sprayed on some of the brick buildings in bold white paint. Unbelievable! It was almost like I was seeing the town I had grown up in for the first time. Well, it had been over thirty years since I lived there, and everything had changed, even the people. I now saw homeless people walking the streets begging, something I had never experienced while living and growing up there. Some were standing around at gas stations, waiting to pump gas for anyone who didn't want to do it for themselves just to make a dollar or two. It didn't seem to matter how much they were paid just as long as they got something for their efforts. Some were hanging around with signs asking for donations, and some were just standing around asking for spare change. I had no explanation for what we were seeing now, but I did explain to Gee how it used to be years back. The only park we had was now all grown up with debris scattered everywhere. It looked very unkept and overgrown. It was in much need of landscaping. Trees had broken limbs, which were just lying around on the ground. The only bench that was there was full of dead leaves, mold, and mildew. It looked more green than silver. The paint was all chipped and peeling with spots of rust showing through. A few homeless people were lying around in the warm heat talking and begging. As we tried walking through the pathway, the smells of urine and body odor were very strong. It was so strong that it made it hard to breathe in the fresh air. I was glad when she said she had seen enough. It was very overwhelming and unsettling to see how rundown the town I had grown up in looked now. I supposed the recession had hit hard in our little town, which caused businesses to move out or close, which also cost a lot of jobs being lost. It looked like the town was struggling hard to get back on its feet. I asked my sister about the state the town was in, and she replied, "You know it's hard to attract new businesses into what seems like a dying town." I had to agree with her on that.

I guess one could say a good home-cooked meal is a must where I'm from, and we had plenty of them while there. Hospitality is what we do best in the South, and no doubt, Gee got the best of what my family and friends had to offer. My hometown might have seen better days, but we had two things to be grateful for: country love and country food.

Chapter 2

We spent a week with my family, and then we were off to her hometown to meet her family. We did a lot of talking as we drove the 673 miles toward Jasper, Missouri. Gee did most of the driving. She said she loved to drive and said she always carried a bag of Skittles with her when she drove long distances because sucking on them kept her awake. I only drove an hour or two at the most to give her a chance to rest her eyes. We mostly talked about my family and how much she enjoyed meeting everyone and how much love was shown to her during her visit. "Your family seems to have a strong bond to each," she said. "Girl, your family loves you very much. I could feel the love." I didn't think too much about that statement at the time because it never occurred to me that her family was going to be that much different from mine.

We also did a lot of stopping along the way to stretch our legs and sometimes to take a long stroll in a park if we saw one from the roadside. We also stopped at different places to have a bite to eat. Cracker Barrel was Gee's favorite. I loved it when we stopped to fill the tank with gas because some of those service stations along the way served hot cooked food. They had the kind of food you just wouldn't eat on a regular basis, but they were great for pigging out on road trips. Our favorite food was fried chicken gizzards. We must have had a ton of them along the way. We ate and sang along with familiar songs we heard on the radio by Aretha Franklin, Lionel Richie, and Stevie Wonder during our road trip to Jasper. It was a fun time; the weather was just right, not too hot and not too cold. It was just the beginning of summer, and the heat waves hadn't set in yet.

In the car with the warm sun beaming through the windshield, I must have dozed off for I was startled when I heard, "Okay, girl, here we are," as we approached the city. "Welcome to Jasper, Missouri, my hometown."

"Wow!" I said. "I must have dozed off for quite a while."

"You did," she said with a smile. "It is now four thirty."

I too smiled as I looked around. I saw tall buildings, fancy billboards, shopping malls, and parks, all the usual things one would see in a big city. From a distance, I could see what looked like the tip of a mountain in the background. The town seemed a little foggy as dawn was settling in, so I wasn't sure. I tried to get a sense of how it must have felt to have lived here through her eyes. In comparison, my hometown was small and country with only two stoplights in the town and mom-and-pop type of stores. It was so small that it seemed everyone knew each other, and over half the people seemed to be related in some way. For me, growing up in Jasper would have been considered big-city living.

Jasper is a small city in southwest Missouri. It had lots of old museums, monuments, and other unique historical factors, things that I had not grown up with in my small town. I had only read about those things in my geography class. The only thing I remember about Missouri was that's where Mark Twain was from. The city was bustling with people, something my hometown was lacking. The population of Jasper was no comparison to my little hometown of Clareville.

As we were driving by, I saw a sign that read "Washington National Park." I asked Gee if we could stop and have a walk in the park before going to her mom's place. She said sure and exited off the road. We found a place to park and got out of the car, stretching our legs. As we entered the gates of the park, there was a beautiful waterfall that looked very inviting. Everything looked clean and pristine; the landscape was lush and well-kept. This was nothing like the park I had taken her to in my hometown. We found an empty bench and sat down, taking in the sights and breathing in the fresh air. People were milling about, some alone, some in groups, and some mothers were walking with baby carriages for exercise. One of the most exciting things about that park was there were no homeless people there. I was in awe of this beautiful land. I had traveled a lot, but to see such small towns and their beauty, you almost had to know someone from them; otherwise, vacationers picked the most popular spots for vacationing and sightseeing.

As we sat people watching, Gee reminisced about her childhood. She had shared with me many stories about her upbringing and what it was like for her growing up there in a small community in the projects. One story I remember was the one she told me about her Uncle Jimmy. She said, "No matter how busy he was, he was never too busy to spend time with me." She was very close to him, and she used to love visiting him because he always had a funny story to tell and a variety of goodies for her, chips, candy, Skittles, etc.

She said with a smile, "I guess that's where I got my love for Skittles from. My uncle loved to dress up. He always looked really sharp in his attire."

She told me he always had lots of company, and she thought that was pretty cool. "Girl, I would see all kinds of people at his place from all over town. They all came driving in fancy cars. Some of the cars had some kind of bushy tail hanging from the rearview mirror. The chrome on the wheels was so shiny you could use them for mirrors." She laughed as she told me that.

"He always had music playing, Sam Cooke, the Platters, Otis Redding. I can hear it now," she said with a smile on her face. "The ladies and men were always dressed up as well. The ladies always looked beautiful with their faces made up, and their hair was perfectly in place. They all had on high-heeled shoes, beautiful elbow-length gloves, and hats and purses that always matched. They were very colorful. I would think to myself, when I get to be a grown woman, I'm going to dress up just like those ladies I had seen at my uncle's house."

Later in life, she found out that the reason he always had lots of people around was because he was kind of the town's bootlegger and those people were his clientele. His house was the speakeasy for the neighborhood.

Chapter 3

The first person I met was Gee's mother, Pattie. We went to her place first because that's where we would be staying at the beginning of our trip. Since this was going to be my first time meeting her mom, I wanted to make sure I got the hostess something that she would enjoy to show my appreciation for allowing me to spend a few nights in her home. I asked Gee if there was anything in particular that her mother would like, and her reply was "liquor." Then she said, "My mother can outdrink a sailor—she would love nothing better."

We saw a small neighborhood liquor store on the way, and we stopped so I could pick up something for her mom. I also decided to get a couple of bottles of wine to go with the dinner that her mother had prepared for us. I got a bottle of white and a bottle of red so we'd have a choice depending what we were having for dinner. While in the liquor store, I asked Gee what her mother's favorite beverage was. She said she liked Jim Beam, so I picked up a couple of bottles of wine for us, a bottle of Jim Beam, and also a six-pack of beer as she said her mother also liked beer. I raised my eyebrows at that but kept my thoughts to myself (beer and Jim Beam)!

I asked, "What beer does she drink?"

Gee said, "It doesn't matter—my mother will drink any kind just as long as it's beer." She said that with a snicker. So I picked up a six-pack of Corona, paid the cashier, and we were on our way to Pattie's place.

As we approached Gee's mom's street, I couldn't help but feel a bit anxious about the woman that I had heard so much about and was about to meet for the first time. I had to wonder if she was as crazy as Gee said she was.

We pulled up to an apartment building and walked up a flight of stairs to a blue door with the numbers 365 on it. That was Gee's mom's apartment. Gee knocked on the door, hollering, "Momma, we are here." The door flew open, and standing on the other side was the infamous Pattie with a glass in her hand. I could see that it wasn't water because of the color.

"Well, it's about time. I thought you would have been here a long time ago," she said. "What took you so long to get here?"

Gee said, "Momma, I stopped and took my friend Ruth for a little tour of the park before coming here."

She stood aside, saying "Come on in," and closed the door behind us. In the background, I could hear the theme song playing from *Sex in the City* on her television set. She must have been watching that and having a drink before we came in.

After the introductions, I thought, *I have finally met Pattie.* She seemed pleasant enough, tall, and fairly well-preserved for a woman in her mid-seventies. I thought the mingle gray hair and the style it was in was a little out of the ordinary, but if that was the style she liked, oh well. Her hair stuck up in some places, which made it looked very uneven. It made me think of the character Dr. Strange, hair kind of all over the place. She walked a little bent over with her arms kind of stuck out from her body behind her.

I must admit her mother did look a little crazy, but I had to reserve judgment until I got to know her a little better. Gee and I went back down to get our luggage. When we returned, she showed me to the room Gee and I would share. The room was small but very neat and clean with twin beds. Both beds had at least five or six dolls on them and an assortment of other stuffed animals. Gee removed all the dolls and stuffed animals and put them away in the closet. I thought it was strange for an elderly woman living alone to have that many stuffed animals, especially when Gee had already told me that none of her grandchildren never spent nights there; they rarely came for visits, and besides, they were all grown by then anyway. There was hardly any room to put a suitcase, so I wedged mine between the foot of the bed and the wall.

When it was time to sit down to eat, I noticed Pattie had already made herself a drink. She had finished cooking dinner, and the table was set. She called us in and said, "Have a seat, eat plenty, and enjoy yourselves!" She had cooked mustard greens, corn bread, turkey wings, sweet potatoes, rice, and gravy, and for dessert, we had peach cobbler. The peach cobbler was mouthwatering delicious; the crust browned just right with the crusty corners curled up makes my mouth water again just thinking of it. I must admit she was an excellent cook.

During dinner, she kept the conversation quite lively with her constant chatter. She asked, "Ruth, how did you and Gee meet?"

I explained to her how we met at the airport. Then she said, "How nice. I came to Bermuda a few times myself, a beautiful island but very small."

No argument there, I thought.

"I guess you guys didn't know each other then," she said.

"We didn't," I said.

Then she said, "Well, how do you like it here so far?"

I replied, "Well, I just got here. I'll let you know in a day or two. But the food is delicious." I noticed that she was constantly pouring herself a drink. Her glass was never empty for too long.

"Don't hesitate to get seconds," she said when I'd finished eating. "Don't be shy—drink up."

I did have two glasses of wine with dinner, but I didn't want to appear ungrateful, so I said, "Pattie, I think all I can do is maybe have another glass of wine, and then I'm going to have to call it a night. I'm kind of tired from the long drive." That part was true. I was getting a bit tired and weary.

I did have one more glass of wine and then retired to the room to get some rest. Usually, I'm a person that falls asleep as soon as my head hit the pillow, but this particular night was different. I had too many thoughts going through my head about the woman I had just met. I wasn't sure if *crazy* was the right word to describe her, but *different* sure fit for now, I thought with a smile. I'd have to study her some more before I could come up with a name that would fit Pattie—if that was possible.

I am an early riser, and being in a strange place was no exception. Glancing over, I noticed that Gee was still asleep. I could tell by the mild, even snoring coming from her. I didn't get up; I just lay there with all kinds of thoughts running through my brain. I couldn't help wondering if Pattie would be any different today than she was yesterday. *Does she drink all day?* I did notice when we first arrived, she already had a drink in her hand, and she did drink quite a bit last night with dinner.

I didn't want to be the first one up, so I waited until I heard Pattie stirring around. By the time I did get up, shower, and got dressed, Pattie was already in the kitchen making breakfast. I could smell the bacon cooking. She had cooked a good old-fashioned Southern breakfast, grits with red-eye gravy, eggs, bacon, and biscuits, and a pot of coffee was on the stove. The aroma really perked up my appetite. Her apartment was small and neat, but the smells were prevalent. I could hardly wait to sit down to have that first cup of coffee. Red-eye gravy was something I hadn't had since I was a child living at home. I didn't know anyone still made that type of gravy any more. Red-eye gravy is just plain brown gravy with a spoonful or two of tomato paste in it to give it the reddish coloring.

Gee got up shortly afterward; I'm sure the aroma of breakfast woke her up. After she got dressed, she joined us in the kitchen. "Good morning," she said. "It really smells good in here. Momma, you have outdone yourself with this breakfast."

As we sat down to that delicious meal, Pattie was just as chatty as she had been the night before. "Sit down," she said. "I'm happy to have you guys visiting." Then as an afterthought, she said, "You know how I love to cook, and I hardly get a chance anymore, no one to cook for. When the grandkids were small, I used to cook all the time for them, but I hardly see them anymore." She sat down and took a sip of her coffee. "Cooking has always been one of my favorite things to do." She seemed a little lost in her thoughts as she spoke.

After breakfast, I got up to help clear away the dishes, and I was stunned by what I saw in the trash. What I realized when I saw the empty bottles and cans was that Pattie had finished off almost all the alcohol. I was completely baffled because she didn't appear to be drunk. We had only finished off one bottle of wine with dinner the night before, which left a whole bottle. Nevertheless, I saw both bottles lying in the trash empty, along with the Jim Beam bottle and a couple of bottles of the beer. I was speechless and could hardly get the words out when I whispered under my breath and asked Gee, "Did your mother drink all that liquor?"

She nodded and whispered, "Apparently so," as she kept clearing away the dirty dishes. I was totally dumbfounded, more because she didn't appear to be drunk at all. I kept thinking, *How could someone drink that much and still function as if they hadn't had a drink at all?*

In the light of day, I took another good look at Pattie, and she actually looked a bit deranged, a little unbalanced or unstable, if you will, with a wild look in her eyes. I'm sure that look had a lot to do with her drinking problem especially for a woman of her age. I watched her closely to see if I was missing something that would indicate that she'd had too much to drink the night before, but I couldn't detect much except for the unsteady way she walked and the strong smell that came from her breath when she talked. When she was talking, her words were a bit slurred, and I had to lean back to avoid the foul smell of alcohol. That smell permeated throughout the room. I was even more baffled and just kind of shook my head. At that moment, I could kind of understand what Gee meant when she said her mother was a little crazy, but she had left out the part that her mother was an alcoholic as well.

I still wasn't sure if *crazy* was the right word to describe her, but she was definitely different from any mother that I had ever met. And she certainly outdrank anyone I had ever met at that age. I guess one could say she was a perfect example of a person who could hold their liquor. She gave that phrase a new meaning.

The last night of our stay with Pattie, Gee and I took her out for dinner, allowing her to choose the restaurant; something so simple seemed to be a huge chore for her. She kept naming different ones, and each one was her favorite. She must have rattled off about five before choosing one. In the end, she chose one that offered a buffet. Once we were seated, she started her chatter again, almost like a nervous chatter. She said, "You know, Gee, whenever I come here, the first thing I'm asked is what do I want to drink?" I noticed her hands shook slightly, and I could hear her tapping her feet under the table. Then she said, "You noticed no one has come over to take our drink order yet?"

Gee said, "Momma, just wait and give them time. We just got seated. Stay calm—they are coming." I could see that Gee was a little agitated, but she tried to stay calm as well.

I didn't say anything, just sat there thinking to myself, *After your binge that first night we were there, I can see why you can hardly wait for a drink.* It couldn't have been more than ten minutes before the waiter came over with menus in her hand. "Good evening, ladies. Welcome to Harley's," she said. "Would you ladies like a menu, or are you eating from the buffet?"

We all told her we'd like to order from the menu.

She passed the menus around and said, "I'll give you some time to look over the menu, but in the meantime, I'll take your drink order if you are ready." Gee and I ordered a glass of wine, and Pattie ordered beer. After she took our drink order, she said, "I'll be back shortly with your drinks." With that comment, she left to give us time to decide what we wanted to eat. I thought for sure Pattie was going to eat from the buffet since she had chosen the place, but she studied the menu very carefully, and I studied her. She chose the most expensive meal on the menu. I guess she wanted to make sure she got our money's worth. The waiter came back, took our food order, and was off again.

She couldn't have been gone more than five minutes when Pattie asked, "How long has it been since that waiter took our order?"

Gee said, "Momma, enjoy your drink and have a little patience. We are not the only table she has." Patience didn't seem to be one of Pattie's strong points.

"Well, it's about time!" Pattie said in a very agitated voice as soon as our food was served. Then she said very nastily, staring at the waiter, "I'll have another beer if you don't mind."

I'm sure the waiter heard the nasty way she talked and the way she acted, but she served our food with a pleasant smile and with a very calm demeanor. After she sat the plates in front of us, she said, "I'll be right back with your beer, ma'am." After she returned with Pattie's beer, she said, "I'll be back in moment to check to see if you need anything else. Enjoy your meal, ladies." With that comment, she walked away.

As soon as the waiter left, Pattie started her chatter. She said, "Gee, you know, I hardly hear from your sister anymore, and those kids of hers act like I don't exist. Now what kind of grandkids are those?"

Gee tried to pacify her by saying, "Well, Momma, you know how this younger generation is—they have their own lives to live."

"Well, I am their grandmother, you know. For God's sake, they could stop by every now and again to check on me or even call," Pattie argued.

"Have you tried calling them?" Gee replied.

That comment must have ruffled her feathers because she said, "Why should I? They are the ones who should be calling me. That sister of yours should've taught those girls some manners when they were young, and my grandson—I don't know where the hell he is—no one mentions his name at all."

Gee was quiet, but Pattie wasn't ready to let things go. "Speaking of grandchildren, you haven't mentioned Amber since you came. Where is she, and what is she doing now?"

"Momma, you must have forgotten. I told you the last time we talked that Amber was living in Mobile, Alabama, with the boys, teaching school and doing well."

Pattie rolled her eyes. "If I had remembered, I wouldn't have asked."

Pattie was all wound up; she talked nonstop during dinner and all the way back to her house. By now, I was tired of listening to her complaining and whining, so as soon as we made it inside, I excused myself and went to the room where we slept, thinking I could hardly wait to get out of there. Morning couldn't come soon enough for me. I didn't feel much like making small talk that night; I just wanted to be left alone to digest the woman I had just met. And trust me, Pattie was a lot to digest.

I did get to see Pattie several more times before leaving Jasper because after we left her house, we spent a few nights at Gee's sister's house. Pattie came over while we were there, and each time I saw her, I could see her in a different light. Sometimes she seemed to be very talkative, and other times, she was a bit on the quiet side, kind of withdrawn like. She seemed to want to talk but seemed as if she had to be very careful what she talked about. I don't think she wanted to alienate Gee, so she had to choose what to say and when to say it. I also noticed her eyes didn't miss much that was going on around her. They were like dancing ladybugs. Her conversations with Gee seemed as if she was always fishing for information. "How long are you guys staying in Jasper?" she asked.

"Momma, I'm not sure. We are just playing it by ear. We are in no hurry. I just wanted Ruth to meet my family and see where I grew up." Then she said in an agitated voice, "I will let you know when we get ready to leave."

"Well, I was just wondering," Pattie said under her breath.

I got the feeling that Pattie liked to stick her nose in other people's business. She constantly wanted to know our next move, where we would be staying, and with whom. She especially wanted to know if and when Gee had planned to see her sister, Mattie, but instead of asking outright, she said, "I guess you do plan on seeing your aunt, huh?"

I was curious as well; it was hard to imagine two Patties.

Chapter 4

The next place we stayed was with Gee's sister, Valerie. When we pulled up in her driveway, I was surprised that it only took us ten minutes to get to her house. I was also a little struck by the fact that she lived so close but didn't stop in to see us while we were visiting with her mom. I'm sure she knew we were there.

Gee knocked on the door, and Valerie opened it, squealing happily, "Gee, how are you? It's been so long since I've seen you. Come in." Once inside, she hugged Gee tightly and again told her how happy she was to see her.

Gee said, "Val, I want you to meet my friend, Ruth."

She grabbed me and hugged me as well, saying with a smile, "Hi, Ruth, how are you? I've heard a lot about you, good of course." I hugged her back, telling her how good it was to finally meet her. It was actually refreshing because I was so ready to leave their mom's place.

Then she asked, "How was your visit with our mom?"

I lied of course, hoping she couldn't read the expression on my face, and said it was good, hoping she wouldn't ask any more questions. She didn't because she and Gee had too much to catch up on. I enjoyed hearing them chattering together like two sisters that truly loved and missed each other. "How are Aunt Mattie and Uncle Pedro?" Gee asked.

"They are doing okay," Valerie replied. "You know they haven't heard from Turk in a while, and Aunt Mattie has been worried about that."

"Is he still into drugs?" asked Gee.

"Yes, as far as I know," answered Valerie. "You know Aunt Mattie doesn't like to talk about him too much, so when I see her, I don't ask. He goes missing for a few months and then he shows up again. This time, though, it's been more than a few months since she last heard from him. Let's just hope everything is all right."

Gee nodded. Then I met Valerie's husband, Willard, and their two daughters. Willard was lounging in an overstuffed chair in the living room, comfortably watching a football game. He did politely get up to greet me. He shook my hand and said, "Ruth, it's good to meet you," but went back to the living room immediately to finish watching the game. I thought, *Just like a man*. The youngest daughter still lived at home although she was an adult.

Again, I immediately got the feeling that there were secrets going on with that family as well, especially the daughter who was still living with her parents. She just seemed a bit strange and very much out of the ordinary. She never really looked at us and seemed fixated on looking up at the ceiling instead. She wore a pair of baggy shorts with the band of her underwear showing and a T-shirt. Once the introductions were over, her attitude showed she could hardly wait to escape.

When Valerie was showing me to the room where I would be sleeping, I noticed a door with a "Keep Out" sign hanging on it. It wasn't hard to imagine whose room that was. I also noticed that while we were there, Gee's niece mostly stayed in her room with the door closed. Usually, inside doors are painted white, but LaDonna's (the niece's name) door was painted black with a bold sign hanging on it that read "Keep Out." I couldn't help but stare every time I passed that door and wondered what was going on in that room behind that closed black door. After the introductions, the youngest daughter wasted no time going back to her room, while the other daughter excused herself, telling her mom she had to get back to work because she was on her lunch break. I didn't get to meet her again.

Valerie was a very gracious host just like her mom. Her house was very neat and clean but much more spacious. Here, Gee and I didn't have to share a room. I had plenty of space for my luggage.

The niece was pleasant enough whenever I did see her, but it would only be for a few minutes at a time. I didn't get to talk to her at all because she kept her distance. Her attitude and her uncooperative behavior gave me the feeling that not only should I keep away from her room but I should keep away from her as well. She looked a little boyish to me with a very short haircut that seemed more befitting for a man than a woman. She must have loved baggy shorts because every time I saw her, that's what she was wearing. Even her body build looked more masculine than feminine, which made me wonder about her sexuality. Rather than making us feel welcome, she just made me feel as if we were intruding and she could hardly wait for us to leave.

One morning, as I was about to grab a cup of coffee, I saw her in the kitchen. "Good morning, LaDonna," I said cheerfully. "How are you this morning?"

"Good morning," she replied. "I'm about to leave. Have a good day." *Well*, I thought, *that conversation was short and sweet*. I hardly got ten words out of her; so much for my efforts. After that, I hardly saw her again. When I did, it was just in passing with a grunt here and there. I had the feeling that she purposely stayed out of our way so she wouldn't have to mingle or talk to us.

Valerie did the wash one day while we were there, and I offered to help fold the laundry. She folded all her daughters' belongings, put them neatly in a laundry basket, and set them aside. I thought if I volunteered to set the laundry basket in her room out of the way, that could be a chance for me to get a sneak peek behind that closed black door. I said to Valerie, "Why don't I just set LaDonna's basket right inside her door? That way, it will be out of the way." She hesitatingly agreed with raised eyebrows. I got the feeling that she really didn't want me to go near that room at all, but I grabbed the basket and walked toward LaDonna's room before she had a chance to change her mind.

I opened that black door cautiously, tiptoed in, and set the basket down. I was too nervous to spend too much time looking around, so I quickly surveyed the room. There were black mini blinds at the windows; black curtains hung over the windows. The room was very dark as it was painted a deep purple. On one wall was a perfect deep red circle. I couldn't help but wonder what that circle meant. Just being in that room gave me an eerie feeling. The room was very neat, bed made; everything was in place. As far as I could see, nothing was out of the ordinary, which was disappointing because I was hoping to see something that would help explain her behavior. I guess the dark room matched her dark mood. I'm not sure if she had a job because she was always in and out of the house.

Gee's sister didn't cook the big meals, but she made us welcome to cook and eat whatever we wanted in the kitchen. We didn't do much with them, just mostly sat around talking, me getting to know them and Gee catching up. We did go to downtown Jasper one day for sightseeing. We spent the day just looking around, taking in the sights. We found a lovely little cafe where we sat outside and had a late lunch while we people-watched. It was a beautiful day to be outside, sunny and bright. Sitting there in such a relaxed atmosphere, I felt myself dozing off. Gee must have noticed as well because she nudged me and said it was time to get moving.

Chapter 5

When I first met Mattie, the other twin, even before the introductions, I thought, *Oh my god, she and Pattie have the same face*. How could they not like each other? As I stood staring, I heard Gee say, "Ruth, this is my Aunt Mattie, my mom's twin sister." I had to close my mouth and swallow before I could say anything.

I reached out my hand and said, "Well, hello, it's so good to meet you." I wanted to say so much more, but I kept my thoughts in check.

Very politely, Mattie said, "Hello, Ruth, how are you?" Then she said with a warm smile, "Gee has talked about you so much I feel as if I already know you." I could hardly take my eyes off that woman. I had to blink to keep from staring. Looking at Mattie was like looking at Pattie; the difference was she didn't have that wild look in her eyes, but she was well-preserved like her sister. Her hairstyle was much neater than Pattie's, and she seemed to be a little more refined. She was very pleasant without the harshness, unlike Pattie. I was also introduced to her husband, Pedro, a short, small-framed man. Mattie was taller than her husband by at least two or three inches, but they stood together and made me feel welcome. She wasn't as talkative as her twin. She invited me to sit down and have a cup of tea. We sat in a very old-looking, outdated living room on an overstuffed floral couch. There was a big crocheted doily thrown over the back of the couch and two matching smaller ones on each arm rest. As a matter of fact, there were doilies all over most of the furniture, even on all the small side tables. I noticed on the kitchen table was a big floral-print tablecloth as well. She had lots of whatnots all around. On one wall, there were pictures of Martin Luther King Jr., President John F. Kennedy, and his brother Bobby Kennedy beside a big cloth picture of Jesus sitting with his disciples eating supper. Everything about her decor was old and dated. While the room was clean and neat, it still had a stuffy feeling about it. From the living room, there was a half wall with a big opening that overlooked the kitchen, which was very tiny and stuffed with kitchen things. There were rugs on top of the dated dark-green shag carpet in the living room unlike Pattie's apartment, which was more updated. Mattie still had an old set of the *World Book Encyclopedia* placed neatly on a bookshelf. The bookshelf had more knickknacks on it than books. Lots of family photos adorned the walls. Framed pictures sat on tables. Everywhere you looked, there were a pair of eyes staring back at you. I noticed the husband, Pedro, didn't do much talking; he just kind of sat there listening to the conversation that Gee was having with her aunt. I sat there staring at the three of them, trying to get a feel for what it must have been like to grow up in this family. Finally, Pedro excused himself and went back to his room. I could hear his TV playing old reruns of *Sanford and Son* in the background, and every now and again, I could hear him chuckle here and there.

"How's your mother doing?" Mattie asked. "You know I don't see her that much anymore."

Gee said, "Momma is Momma—she's doing good. We spent a few days with her, and if we hadn't left when we did, we each would have gained ten pounds." We both laughed.

"You know how she loves to cook."

Mattie said, "Yes, I remember how she love to cook, but I really don't see her much anymore. Every now and again, I might run into her at the grocery store and we talk a little, but she seems to always be in a hurry. How is she? I have tried calling her several times, but she never answers, and she never calls back."

"She's doing fine," Gee said, "still drinking too much, but you know how she loves her alcohol." Mattie acknowledged that comment with a nod. We stayed about another half hour and then got up to say our goodbyes to leave.

"It was good meeting you guys and thanks for the tea," I said. Mattie called out to Pedro to come say goodbye. Again, he was very gracious in his mannerism.

In the car, headed back to Valerie's house, I asked Gee, "How is it possible that those two can't get along? They look so much alike." I was thinking if it wasn't for their mannerisms, no one could tell them apart.

"I don't know," Gee said, "but as far back as I can remember, they have always squabbled about something. It's usually Momma that provokes the chaos—that I do know."

I was thinking, *Umm, I can see that*. But I thought Mattie was still a little too reserved. I didn't want to read too much into Mattie and Pedro because I hadn't known them long enough or spent enough time with them to inject too much. Their demeanor did seem much more stable, and while Mattie may have had the same face as her twin, their personality was definitely different. Pattie was much more talkative and seemed to be much more unpredictable than Mattie.

That night at Valerie's house, I just couldn't fall asleep. As I lay in bed that night, my mind was racing trying to comprehend the people I had met so far. I tossed and turned but at some point must have finally fallen into an exhausted sleep. The next morning, instead of having coffee at Valerie's house, I asked Gee if she would like to go out for coffee. "Of course," she said, "that would be great. Let's go to Panera's. They have good coffee and a very good pecan coffee roll." She knew how much I liked pecans. This would also give us the opportunity to talk in private, and I could ask questions without the fear of being overheard that had been building up in my mind.

Once we had gotten our coffee, we found a table outside as the morning sun was beautiful and sat down. As soon as I took my first sip of coffee, I started asking questions about some of the things I had witnessed and heard in different conversations with different family members.

"Gee," I said, "when we were at Mattie's house, I noticed that her husband didn't do much talking. Is that how he always is? I also noticed he did seemed a bit antsy. He seemed more interested in hearing what was being said without his participation. I just got the feeling he wanted to make sure nothing was being said that shouldn't be—if you know what I mean."

"He's kind of always been that way. He's never been a very talkative man," she said.

"How many children do they have?" I asked.

"They had four, one daughter and three sons. Two of the sons are dead," she said. I perked up at that statement. "What happened to the two sons that died?"

"Marcus, her oldest son, died of AIDS even before we knew a lot about the disease at that time. He was gay."

"So what happened to the other son?"

"His name was Jason, and he jumped off a bridge and killed himself."

"Wow!" I said. "That had to have been very traumatic I would think."

"It was," she said. "It took Aunt Mattie a long time to get over his death if she ever did. I don't think my uncle ever really got over losing his sons because after their death is when he started drinking heavily."

"Was there a suicide note or anything?" I asked.

"No, nothing that would have given them closure or helped them to understand why he did what he did."

"Where is the daughter?" I asked.

"She moved away after college to another state and never came back," she said.

"How far apart were the two sons' death?"

"I think they were about three years apart—if I'm not mistaken," she said.

Wow! I kept repeating to myself, *This family has been through a lot*. Maybe that explained the vibes I was getting from Pedro because he seemed very sincere but very withdrawn at the same time. He seemed like he was with us and not with us if you know what I mean. Or maybe he wanted to make sure there were no family secrets spilled during the conversation, especially while a stranger was present.

I asked, "So what's happening with the third son, Turk?"

She said, "He's around someplace. He got into drugs heavily after the death of his brothers, but the last time I heard anything about him, he was in rehab trying to overcome his addiction." Then as an afterthought, she said, "I'll have to remember to ask Valerie about Turk—that's his nickname. His real name is Terrance, but as a child, he got stuck with being called Turk."

I had other questions that I made a mental note of, but for now, I pushed them aside, and we just enjoyed our breakfast while basking in the morning sun. It was so relaxing and refreshing.

I enjoyed the fresh aroma of my coffee and the pecan roll. I did ask, "Whom are we visiting next?"

She said, "I think we should go visit with Aunt Cida. She lives relatively close by, and we can spend some time there before checking into our hotel." Well, I knew it was getting close to the time that we would be leaving Jasper, but I wanted to make sure I got to see as many of her relatives as possible. Her uncles no longer lived in Missouri; she said they had moved to some town in North Carolina years ago. I felt a bit disappointed not being able to compare the girls to the boys, but I knew we wouldn't be going to North Carolina anytime soon—if ever. We both still lived in Bermuda and at some point had to make our way back. One thing I can say for sure, her family was a lot more interesting and colorful than mine.

Just as we were about to leave, we heard a loud motorcycle pull up. The guy got off the bike and started walking toward us. It was hard to see his face because he was wearing a helmet. He came right over to our table, pulled off his helmet, and said, "Hello, ladies, how are you?"

Gee jumped up and screamed, "CJ, is that you? Oh my god, it is. I can't believe this."

CJ was a big guy. I could hear the excitement in her voice. He then grabbed Gee in a bear hug, lifting her off the ground. "Girl, where have you been? I heard you were coming into town. It's really good to see you," he said. For a moment, they were so caught up in each other until I thought they had forgotten I was sitting there.

She then said again, "Oh my goodness! I can't believe you are here." She was smiling from ear to ear and so was he. "How did you find us, and how did you even know I was in town?"

Still standing holding her, he said, "I have always kept up with your whereabouts through your sister, and when she told me that you would be coming for a visit, I just made sure I would be around to surprise you."

Then she turned to me and said, "CJ, this is my good friend Ruth."

I got up to extend my hand, but he grabbed me and hugged me as well. "Hi, Ruth, it's good to meet you." Then he added, "Your name is pretty popular among Gee's family. I heard a lot about you."

I was a little taken aback, but I said, "Thank you very much for the compliment."

Well, I could clearly see that he and Gee needed some time alone because they were just standing there staring at each other with smiles on their faces, so I excused myself and went inside with the pretense of having to use the bathroom. As I glanced back, he and Gee seemed engrossed in their conversation. I smiled to myself as I entered the door to the restaurant. I also got another cup of coffee and found a seat inside to give them some alone time. I sat near a window where I could watch the two of them together. I thought, *They must be catching up as old friends usually do when they haven't seen each other in a few years.* Finally, Gee beckoned for me to come out and say goodbye to CJ.

After the visit with her friend CJ, Gee called her Aunt Cida. "Good morning, Aunt Cida. How are you this morning?"

She must have said "Good morning" back because Gee told her we were in town, and she had a friend that she wanted her to meet. We paid our bill, and off we went to Cida's house. On the way there, Gee pointed out things of interest and old landmarks in the town. "We will take a tour of where I grew up later in the day if we have time," she said.

We pulled up to a much larger apartment complex than where her mom lived, and I asked, "Is this where Cida lives?" I was kind of surprised to see that she lived in an apartment as well.

"Yes," Gee said, "and so do her son and grandson." She hadn't mentioned them before, but I was looking forward to meeting them. We entered the building, got on the elevator, and went up to the third floor. Gee knocked on door number 15. So far, Mattie was the only one of the sisters who owned her own home. An elderly lady, maybe in her eighties, opened the door. She was dressed up; her wig was well-groomed, but it did sit a little crooked on her head. I had to fight the urge to set it straight.

She said, "Come in, child. Come on in. How are you?"

Gee gave her a big hug as she said, "Aunt Cilda, how are you? You look, well, beautiful as ever. I want you to meet my friend Ruth."

I extended my hand as I said, "Hello, Mrs. Johnson. It's good to meet you."

Cida invited us in. "Have a seat, you two. Could I offer you some coffee, hot tea, or something?" We both said no as we just had finished having coffee with breakfast.

Gee said, "No, Aunt Cida. We just stopped by to see you. We just finished having breakfast, and I'm all coffee out."

After we were seated, I noticed how small and cramped her apartment was. It was old and dated like her sister Mattie but more cramped. One thing the sisters did have in common was neatness. We could barely move around as she had more than enough furniture in the small living room, but everything had a place. As we sat on the couch, our knees almost touched the coffee table. I noticed, like her sister, she had even more what-nots scattered around her apartment. There was hardly any vacant space as far as I could see. Her apartment was kind of dark with a slight musty smell to it. I had to almost strain my eyes to see anything. She had one small lamp lit, but it didn't give off much light. Once we were seated and my eyes got adjusted to the dark room, I could see a layer of dust on most of her furniture. I guess at that age, who cares?

Cida asked, "What brought you this way, Gee? It's been a while since I last seen you. Are you still living on that island?"

"Yes," Gee said, "I'm still living in Bermuda. I'm just here visiting."

"Ruth and I decided to take a trip together so we could meet each other's family. We were in Mississippi last week where I met her family, and from there, we drove here so she could meet my family."

"That's nice," Cida said. "Mississippi, huh? It's been many moons since I heard of anybody from that state. Is it still like what we hear on television? When I think of Mississippi, I think of it as Klansmen territory." She said this with a smirk. "I guess most people my age would."

I wasn't sure how to answer that, so I said, "Well, I guess it depends on where you live and how you get along with the people you live with in the town. It's been many years since I lived there, and everyone seems to get along fine. I'm sure there are some Klansmen still living there, but by now, they know to keep to themselves."

Then Cida asked, "Child, have you seen the twins yet?"

"Yes," Gee said, "we spent a few days at Momma's, left there, and spent a few days with Valerie and her family. We just about seen everyone but you and your family."

Then Gee asked, "Where's Sonny and his son? Are they are still living next door?"

Cida said, "Yes, they are still living next door. Where in the world would they go now? They been living there for years now. I think they are home. Haven't heard from them this morning, but they should be there."

Before leaving, I asked Cida if I could use her bathroom. "Of course," she said, "it's right through that door to the left." As I made my way to the door she pointed toward, I noticed the hallway had pictures lined each side of the wall. I stepped into the bathroom and had to literally feel for the light switch because so much stuff was on the walls, even in the bathroom. This was one of the times a small flashlight would have been handy, I thought. When I returned to the living room, I heard Gee say, "On our way out, we will stop in to see them."

We stayed for about an hour, and I kind of halfway listened to Gee and her aunt talking and catching up with family matters. I was more curious about how these people lived and why they didn't visit each other although they all lived in the same town, just barely minutes from each other. As I looked around Cida's apartment, I could see that nothing had been updated in that place for years. Like her sister, she still had the same floral-patterned sofa, only she had a plastic covering on hers. I found it kind of funny that they didn't visit each other, but they seemed to have the same taste in decorating. So far, Gee's mom was the only one seemed to have left the sixties and seventies behind. Then I remembered Gee telling me that her and her sister had redone their mother's apartment a few years back after they finally got her to move away from the area where they had grown up in. Cida even had the lamp fixture on a chain hanging from the ceiling. I had to smile at that as I hadn't seen one of those in years. I guess I was lost in thought because suddenly, I heard Gee say, "Aunt Cida, it's been good seeing you, but we need to get going. We are all meeting for dinner tonight. Are you coming?"

"I don't think so, child. I don't go out much anymore, maybe to the grocery store to do a little shopping, but that's about it. You guys go and enjoy each other. I've had my visit with you." Then as an afterthought, she said, "Say hi to everybody for me."

Gee told her she would and looked over at me and asked, "Are you ready?" I nodded my response as I got up to shake hands with Cida.

After we left Cida's place, we went next door and knocked on Sonny's door, but no one answered. We made our way back to the car and from there headed to the hotel to check in.

"Gee, how many children does Cida have?" I asked.

"She has five," she said.

"Where's the husband?" I asked.

"Oh, he died about ten years ago."

"Look, girl, I have a different family from most," she said with a laugh.

"My mom and all her siblings had at least one gay or lesbian child, and some even have gay and lesbian grandchildren," she said. "My younger sister Pat is a lesbian, but you won't get to meet her on this trip because she lives in Hawaii."

"My Aunt Mattie had a gay son, and Aunt Cida has a bisexual son, Sonny. Sonny's son is gay. Aunt Cida other son, Martin, has two sons, and they both are gay. Her daughter Yogi has two girls, and one is a lesbian, and the other one has a child by a distant cousin. My family has so many issues until I can't figure them all out myself."

"Why did Cida and her husband name their daughter Yogi?" I asked, thinking that was an unusual name for a girl.

"Her husband used to love cartoons, and Yogi Bear was one of his favorite cartoon characters, so he named his daughter Yogi. Now you see what I mean about having a different family."

"What was his name?" I asked.

With a laugh, she said, "His name was Sam. He did name his youngest son Sammie, whom I haven't seen in ages. I'm not sure if he still lives in Jasper or not. I will have to ask Yogi about him tonight when I see her."

She said they, meaning the cousins, had all moved around quite a bit, and it was hard to keep up with them all.

I have nothing against one's sexual preference, but I did find it a bit strange that five siblings would each have a gay or lesbian child. I found that unusual. I had a lot to think about after meeting Gee's aunts. I did wonder where the gay gene came from.

Chapter 6

We went back to Valerie's house to get our things and say our goodbyes. If LaDonna was there, we didn't get to see her or say goodbye to her, which by now was not unusual. I had a lot to digest after those visits. Her family did seem to be a tangled mess, but family is family after all, and most families have some tangles in it.

We made our way to the hotel, checked in, and decided afterward to do some sightseeing before going out for dinner. While Jasper was a pretty large city, the area where Gee grew up was a very small community within the city. On the drive there, she pointed out the city's library, the courthouse, the city hall, and other things of interest. Once we got on the street that led to her community, she said, "This is it!" She then pulled over to a small parking area where we just sat in the car, staring as she seemed to be taking everything in around her as though she were seeing it for the first time. I kept quiet, but I did notice the expression on her face as she seemed lost in her own thoughts.

Finally, she said, "Girl, it's been a long time since I've come back here, and wow, how things have changed!"

I saw a flash of excitement in her eyes as she pointed. "Over there is where we used to shop for groceries. We had everything we needed right here in this little community, a laundromat, grocery store, movie theater, a church, and a drugstore—we had it all. The drugstore was owned by the Anderson family."

"I wonder if any of the Andersons are still around?" She said this out loud, but it seemed as if she were talking to herself. "It was not only the drugstore. It was the place where we all hung out on the weekends. Every child in our neighborhood hung out at the drugstore. If anyone was looking for a missing child, they could always find them sitting at the counter in Anderson's Drugstore." Then as an afterthought, she said, "What memories!"

I noticed this was the same park we'd seen when we drove in but had no idea it was where she grew up because it had no resemblance to what she was describing now. I could also see that mountain again, so I asked, "What's that mountain called over there?" as I pointed.

"Oh, that's Mount Washington. That's who our little community was named for," she said.

"It's hard to imagine that all of that is gone and this area is built up with houses and apartment buildings now." She said they (meaning a group of the grown-ups) had even renamed our little village. It was called Washington Heights after the first president. I thought that was impressive. She said to me but more to herself, "I remember during the week in the summer, as soon as we finished doing chores, we would gather at our house to watch TV. Around eleven o'clock was gathering time. We would start out watching the soap opera *All My Children* and didn't stop watching TV until *Dark Shadows* went off." As an afterthought, she said, "Those were the good times."

I didn't do much talking, but I did a lot of listening as I was thinking to myself, this family definitely was not the traditional family that I was used to. On a hot summer day, we would be outside playing until dark, not inside watching TV.

"Our yard used to be full of children," she continued. "That's where I met my close friend CJ. He lived next door to us. We remained friends throughout the years. Whenever I came back to visit my family, we always spent some time together, catching up." I could look at her face and tell by the tone of her voice that she was remembering those times. She smiled to herself. "Once we both got married, we kind of went our separate ways. I never forgot him, just kind of pushed memories of him aside. We were childhood friends, and he will always be special to me."

We got out of the car and took a walk through the park that she used to play in. The park now was landscaped with lush green grass, benches, and picnic tables. It had walking and bicycle trails. "None of that existed when I lived here," she said. "It was just a park where we children played." I could tell just from the tone of her voice that this place held a lot of memories for her. "Girl, the grass was never this green and lush because we played so hard it hardly grew," she said smiling. I walked along with her quietly, listening whenever she saw a landmark that triggered a memory. She said, "Right over there used to be a little white church that we attended. I wonder whatever happened to the families that used to go there. Father Daniels was our pastor, and I'm not sure what happened to him after we moved."

Again, as if talking to herself, she said, "Every child in our neighborhood had to get dressed up and attend church on Sundays, no acceptations unless someone was ill." She then smiled to herself. "We couldn't wait to get home to pull off those church clothes and put on our play clothes to go outside. Playing outside was one of the big highlights of our time besides sitting at the counter in the drugstore sipping a soda."

We found an empty bench, where we sat just enjoying the scenery around us. We must have sat there for more than two hours or so, not saying much before we finally got up to leave. By the time we were leaving, we saw people coming to walk the trails, some with small children in strollers, some with pets, some on bicycles, some on skateboards, and some just sitting on the benches enjoying the sunshine. It was another beautiful day to be outside.

On our way back to the hotel, I asked, "What are we doing next?" She then told me that we were going out for dinner with some of her other relatives that I hadn't met yet. She said it was going to be about fifteen of them and we were all meeting at a restaurant later that evening. She mentioned that I would get to meet Cida's children and some of her grandchildren.

Once we got in our room, we decided to rest up before heading back out for dinner. I was tired but couldn't sleep, so I lay down just to rest. I was still trying to put faces with names of the ones I had already met and to file each one in a mental box for later. I must admit that Gee's family was definitely different from most traditional ones that I've met. They all were very gracious and nice but still different. The one thing I did notice was that I could see resemblance in the sisters' mannerism, but I hadn't seen or met anyone that looked like Gee. If one didn't know that the people I had met were her family, you wouldn't know by looking because Gee's face had no resemblance to anyone that I had met so far. As some would say, she seemed to be the odd one out.

The one person I didn't hear Gee speak of was her father. I wanted to ask about him, but the timing wasn't right. We both needed to rest up before getting ready for the dinner.

As we made our way to the restaurant that night for dinner, I was a bit overanxious to meet the family members that I hadn't met. We pulled into the parking lot of the restaurant and found a place to park. Gee spotted someone getting out of their car at the same time we were. She hollered out, "Hey, Yogi, how are you?" I got out of the car and watched as they swiftly walked towards each other and embraced each other affectionately.

"Wow, it's been a long time since I last saw you," Gee said.

"I know, how have you been?" asked Yogi.

"Doing well, what about you?"

Yogi replied, "I've been doing good, still working at the same hospital. I've been there for twenty-plus years now. I've been thinking about retiring but never quite get around to it. You know how that is."

"Gracie is still in school, and Roz has decided to go back. It never ends," she said. "You know how we mothers are—we never stop helping." With that comment she laughed.

"Yes, I know," Gee said. "I'm glad my daughter has finally finished, and now she's working, teaching school in Mobile, Alabama."

"That's great," said Yogi. "How is Amber? It's been years since I last seen her."

"How many children does she have now?"

"She's doing good. We talk almost every day, sometimes twice a day."

"She has two boys—the oldest is six and the youngest is three."

And then she said, "Yogi, I want you to meet my friend Ruth."

I extended my hand and said, "Hi, it's good to meet you."

"Same here," she said. "I've heard so much about you."

I smiled and said, "All good I hope."

"Of course," she said.

We started walking toward the restaurant with Gee and Yogi still talking. Once inside Gee explained to the hostess that we were meeting a big party and gave the name. The hostess said, "Sure, right this way please." We followed her to a table that already had about twelve people sitting down. I must admit I felt a little tongue-tied as I looked around at faces I hadn't seen before. The only familiar faces I saw were Gee's mother, her sister Valerie, and her husband, Willard. I made my way over to where they were sitting and sat down in the empty chair next to Pattie.

"Hello, Ruth, how are you?" she said. "It's good to see you again."

"Hello to you, Pattie," I said. "It's good to see you again as well." I was thinking to myself, *That remains to be seen as the night wears on.* I was remembering her drinking. Gee did all the introductions and ended it with, "Everybody, this is my friend Ruth."

There was no way I was going to remember all those names, so I just tried to make mental notes of something about each person to associate them with a name if I could remember. Everyone was chatting with each other as if they hadn't seen each for a long time. They seemed to be catching up and trying to distinguish what had been going on with them since the last time they saw each other. The noise sounded like a swarm of bees buzzing nonstop. There's was no way any particular conversation could be established, so I just sat there listening. Pattie seemed a bit on the quiet side as well, which was surprising for I remembered how talkative she was when I first met her. Her eyes still had that wild look in them as she scanned the faces around her. As we sat down, I guess I was doing the same thing Pattie was doing, scanning the faces around me. I was mainly trying to see a face that resembled Gee's. I made a mental note to have a conversation with her about that.

When the waiter approached us to start taking orders for drinks, everyone stopped talking long enough to give her their order.

Of course, Pattie ordered a beer. I ordered wine, and most of them just ordered ice tea or a soda. With the drinks ordered, the waiter left saying she would be back soon. As soon as she walked away, the noise started back. I looked around the restaurant. Although it was quite full, our table seemed to be the most noisy one. I have to admit everyone seemed as if they had genuinely missed each other and they seemed really happy to see each other again. Yogi and Gee seem engrossed in their own private conversation. Cida's son Sonny and his two sons were there. Sonny was a huge guy, tattooed to boot. He had on a rainbow sleeveless T-shirt under his black leather jacket with a two-headed lion on the back with Missouri pride on the bottom. I couldn't help but stare at his tattoos. They were on his neck, the back of his hand, and when he pulled his jacket off, both arms were filled with tattoos. Those would be what is referred to as a sleeve today. His black leather boots matched his leather jacket. He certainly didn't look like the rest of the clan in his attire, but that must have been the way he usually dressed because no one looked surprised at all. They all embraced him and told him how happy they were that he was able to join them.

Yogi asked, "What about Mama? Is she coming, Sonny?"

He replied, "No, he said she didn't feel up to it, so I just left her alone."

I thought, *He must be pretty warm in all that leather*, because the weather was still a bit warm and humid.

It was hard to carry on any conversation with them as they all seemed to be talking to each other. Yogi's two daughters were there, Gracie and Roz. Most of the people there were Cida's children and grandchildren. Gee's sister Valerie and her husband came, but neither of her daughters were there. I overheard Valerie asking, "Momma, are you all right? You seemed to be very quiet tonight."

"Yes, I'm fine," she said. "Just trying to take it all in. It's been a while since I last saw everyone."

"It's been a while since I have seen everyone as well," Valerie said.

"Willard and I don't get out much these days, and when we do, we usually kind of stay on our side of town."

Then Valerie asked, "Where's Aunt Mattie and Uncle Pedro?"

"I have no idea," said Pattie. "I don't even know if they were invited or not."

"I'm sure they were. Maybe they just couldn't make it," Valerie said.

"Maybe so," said Pattie, "but I'm sure they didn't come because they knew I'd be here—you know how your Aunt Mattie is."

"Now, Momma, don't think like that. I'm sure they had another reason for not coming."

Pattie muttered under her breath, "Yeah, right!"

By then, the drinks came, and it took three waiters to bring them all. It must have taken about ten minutes to get them all passed out and to make sure everyone got what they ordered. Pattie was the only one who ordered beer, so she made sure she got the correct one. We all held our drinks up and toasted each other. The food had been preordered, and thank goodness because that would have been a disaster. Once the food came, we all starting eating, but the chatter kept going with each one trying to talk over the other. I could only pick up bits and pieces of their conversations. It was too many different ones going on at the same time to stay focused on one. I have to say, it was a fun night. I can't say I got to know anyone, but they all seemed to have enjoyed each other. As we got up to say our goodbyes, they all made promises to stay in touch and not allow so much time go by without seeing each other again.

On the way back to the hotel, Gee and I did little talking as we both were too tired. It had been a long day, and we just needed to get to bed as we were leaving the next morning. I leaned back on the headrest, closed my eyes, and just tried to relax my brain. Questions could wait; for now, I just needed to rest, and I could tell Gee did to because she's usually the talkative one, but she was quiet on the ride back.

Chapter 7

The next morning, as we were preparing to leave, I told Gee how much I enjoyed meeting and getting to know her family. We made small talk as we packed and checked around the hotel room to make sure we weren't leaving anything behind. We made our way downstairs to the lobby, dragging our luggage, still a bit tired. We paid the bill and left on our way back to Georgia for a few days and then back home to Bermuda.

On the way to the car, Gee said she wanted me to meet one more of her relatives, her aunt on her dad's side. She said we wouldn't stay long, just pop in to say hi and be on our way. I told her that was fine by me. She called her Aunt Thelma and told her she was in Jasper and asked if it would be okay if she stopped by with a friend for a quick visit. Her aunt must have said yes because as we drove out of the hotel parking lot headed to her aunt's house. Gee said, "I'd hate to be this close and not go see my aunt as she getting on in age." I assured her it was fine. It's not like we had to be any particular place at a certain time.

We drove up to a little small white frame house that was a bit rundown. The house sat very close to the sidewalk, and as we got closer, I could see that it was badly in need of a paint job. There was some type of wire fencing around the front of the house, and it had a very old metal gate for the entrance. The overgrown lawn was full of weeds. It looked like it hadn't been mowed in months. As a matter of fact, just driving by the dwelling looked as if it had been unoccupied for years. Gee wrestled with the rusted lock until she finally got it opened. She left the gate ajar so when we left, she wouldn't have to wrestle with it again. We had to weave our way through the weeds and overgrown grass to get to the steps that led to the front door. The steps were very unsafe, very creaky with holes in them. We literally had to watch every step we took.

Gee knocked on the front door, and we heard a woman's frail voice called out to us, "Come in." Gee opened the door, which made a loud, creaky sound. We entered into a tiny living room that was cramped with furniture. This living room was worse than Gee's Aunt Cida. Her Aunt Thelma offered us a seat. "Sit down, chile. How are you doing?" Gee and I exchanged glances, wondering where we would sit. We literally had to walk sideways, taking one step at a time to get in. She was sitting in a wheelchair off to the side surrounded by clutter. The couch had so much stuff on it I didn't see how we could possibly sit on it. Gee arranged some things and moved some stuff off it so we could find a little space to sit, very uncomfortably, I might add. There was absolutely no room in that house to turn around, and her aunt, being a frail older woman, should not have been living there under those conditions. As I was sitting there, I wondered how she could maneuver a wheelchair in this house. I did notice that she had a walker next to the wheelchair, so I assume when she got out of the chair, she used the walker. Again, I couldn't see how, so I gave up and focused on the conversation Gee was having with her aunt.

She asked Gee if she had seen her family, and Gee told her what we had been doing since we came and the people she had visited. As I looked around, I saw a chair lift on the stairway, which meant her aunt had to get in that lift to get upstairs to her bedroom. This cramped little house surely was not designed for a person with any kind of disability. We didn't stay very long as we needed to get on the road. Besides, I was more than ready to get out of that house. I don't think I had ever been in a house that was so cramped with so much stuff. Her aunt was a hoarder in the worst way possible. We said our goodbyes and got up to leave. I was thinking to myself, *We have to make our way back down those rickety old steps again.* Going down seemed worse than going up. Gee and I held onto each other, carefully watching every step we took.

As we made our way back out that dilapidated old metal gate, I asked Gee, "How does your aunt stay in that house by herself? That house isn't safe for anyone, let alone a handicapped person."

Gee replied, "Well, she's been there as long as I can remember, and I don't think she would ever consider moving at this stage of her life. She seems to have made everything work for her in whatever way she needed it to. She doesn't have any children, so there's no one to come see about her because all her close relatives are dead."

She said as an afterthought, "It's sad but true."

We drove for about an hour before stopping at a Cracker Barrel for breakfast. Once we got seated, I asked Gee about other relatives on her father's side because everyone I had met besides Aunt Thelma was from her mother's side of the family. She said she didn't really know any of the other relatives because growing up, she didn't spend any time with her father's family. She then said, "I don't think any of them ever owned me, and some of them probably didn't know I even existed. Aunt Thelma was the only one that ever reached out to me—that's why I try and go see her whenever I'm here." I glanced up and saw that the expression on her face was a sad one as she spoke.

Then she made a statement that really floored me. "I don't even know if the man my mother said was my father was really true or not. I always wondered if he was because I only saw him a few times while growing up, and he never really acted like he was my dad. On the occasion I did see him, he would speak and ask how I was doing, but that's about all. I just know that after he got married and had a family of his own, I never seen him again. That's why I'm not sure if his family even knew about me." I thought about my relationship with my father, and I just couldn't imagine how that felt. Gee fell silent again as she must have been deep in thought.

We finished our breakfast in silence, paid our bill, and left but not before Gee got her bags of Skittles. In the car, I closed my eyes to rest and think about all the characters I had met on that short trip as I tried sorting them out in my mind. There was nothing traditional about Gee's family. I could see how she thought my family was very close and how she could feel the love my family had for each other. Her family was so different from any family I had ever met; the only way I could describe them were characters that you read about, not ones you live with. I finally dozed off for some much-needed sleep.

Chapter 8

On the drive back to Georgia, Gee seemed very quiet. I struck up a conversation. "Gee, you are so quiet. What are you thinking about?"

"Just thinking about my old hometown and how my little community had changed," she replied. "Although I have gone back several times over the years, I had never visited my old neighborhood like I did this time. Usually when I come here, I stay with Momma and visit my sister, my aunt, and a few other relatives but never had the time—or should I say, I never took the time—to visit my old haunts. I'm only there for a few days, and that's usually for a holiday or some special occasion—you know what I mean."

I nodded, not really knowing what else to say.

We drove on in silence for a while, both of us kind of lost in our own thoughts. I had a few questions I wanted to ask, but I was waiting for the right moment. I wanted to give her time to think and relish her thoughts before I bombarded her with more questions. She had mentioned her father, Jerome Monroe, several times, but I wanted to make sure the timing was right to ask her a few questions about him. I was curious as to why she didn't ask her Aunt Thelma about him since that was the only relative of his that we visited. I also noticed that while we were at her aunt's house, there were no family photos that I could see, but it was so overcrowded in that little house, so if there were any photos, I probably wouldn't have seen them anyway.

We must have driven about an hour before I decided to start a conversation.

"Gee," I said, "why didn't you ask your aunt about the man that was supposed to be your father?" After all, Thelma was his sister, so I thought that was a valid question.

"Well, Ruth," she said, "that's a long story." She hesitated for a moment before going on. "Girl, I don't know where to start." Well, she really piqued my curiosity then.

"I'm not sure where to start," she stated again. "You remember my Aunt Mattie?"

"Of course," I said, thinking to myself, *How could I forget her?* As a matter of fact, how could I forget any of the people I had met? They all were unforgettable characters as far as I was concerned.

"Well, Aunt Mattie told me that she wasn't sure if Jerome was my father or not because he was engaged to some other woman. I can't even remember her name, but anyway, the story I was told was he and this woman had a fight one night, and he went out got drunk and in retaliation ended up having a one-night stand." At that statement, my ears perked up. I wanted to ask who, but I figured out who even before she told me.

"The one-night stand was my mother, and guess who was a product of that one-night stand?"

I didn't know what to say. I just kind of swallowed and tried to think of something to say that would lighten the mood, but my mind drew a blank. What do you say to something like that? I was completely at a loss for words. There was a long moment of silence before either of us could speak. Finally, she spoke.

"Now you see why I say the things I do about my mother." Silence again.

"You don't know how many times I wanted to ask my mother about that story, but I have to keep quiet because Aunt Mattie told me I could never mention it because my mother would flip out. Aunt Mattie said she's not sure if Momma even knows she know about the one-night stand because she didn't tell her. He did." Another moment of silence. Then out of the blue, she said, "I have spent my whole life looking for a face that looks like mine."

Well, I didn't know what to say to that because all the faces that I had seen so far didn't have any resemblance to her face. After that statement, her mood changed; it felt heavy, so I just leaned my head back on the headrest and closed my eyes. I knew she needed to talk about her past, and I needed to listen, but with so many thoughts clogging up my brain, I just needed to try to sort them out before I could say any more on that subject. This was something so personal I was wondering what I could say that wouldn't make her mother look worse than she already was in Gee's eyes.

By now, we had to have a break, so we started looking for a place to pull over, just to stretch out legs and get some fresh air. I looked up and saw that big sign advertising Cracker Barrel. I excitedly said, "Look, Gee, there's another Cracker Barrel sign that says the next one is only two miles ahead. Maybe we can stop there, grab something to eat, and stretch our legs." Well, she was definitely on board for that.

It was lunchtime, and the place was crowded. It was a bit of a wait. We browsed in the store until our buzzer went off. After we were seated, I asked, "Gee, are you all right?"

"Yes," she said, "still trying to digest the events of this trip, things that I hadn't thought about for a long time, things that I had just pushed back so far in mind that I didn't allow myself to think about whenever I visit my family."

Looking at her face, I said, "Well, you know what, we don't have to talk about those things right now. Let's just eat our lunch and talk about happier things like getting a bag of skittles before we leave." That made her laugh. We ordered our food and ate in silence, paid our bill, and got up to go.

Chapter 9

Once we got back in the car, I tried to think of something to say that would lighten up the mood before she went quiet again. So I said, "Gee, you know, if we didn't have some craziness going on in our families, we wouldn't have much to talk about, huh?" That brought a smile to her face. "I'm sure there were a lot of things that went on in my family that I don't know about because we weren't allowed to be around when grown-ups were talking. The minute they wanted to talk about something that we were not supposed to hear we were sent outside to play. Girl, they sometimes didn't have to say anything, just give you that look, and we knew what that look meant." Gee managed another small smile, but I could tell she was still thinking about all that she had encountered on this particular trip.

On the drive back, we stopped for gas and of course got those delicious fatty fried chicken gizzards, and they were some kind of tasty as well as greasy. We had the music playing loud, singing to the songs we knew and making up words when we didn't know what they were saying. It was just as much fun going back as it was coming. It was a long drive but a pleasant one.

Once we got back to Gee's house in Georgia, it was getting close to the time we should be making plans to head back to Bermuda. Somewhere along the way, I decided to write a story about the people I had met. I remember Gee telling me about another sister of hers that had died due to a car accident, but we hadn't gotten into that during this trip. Apparently, she was the youngest child. I didn't want to bombard her with more questions, so I'd give it a day or two before approaching anything more to do with her family.

We both were lazy and slow about making our plans to return to our other home. Being in the United States had a certain appeal to it after being away for so long. We could go shopping because there were so many choices. We could go out to breakfast or dinner or do whatever we felt like doing for the most part. The choices were endless. Everything seemed so inexpensive compared to what things cost in Bermuda. I think during that time, the Walmart stores were the most exciting. It had such a vast variety of goods. There were no places on the island to do that kind of shopping.

A few days later, as we were sitting around in the kitchen drinking coffee and talking, I asked Gee if anything was bothering her. I could sense that she had a lot on her mind because she was a lot quieter than usual. Gee has always been a very talkative person, and this quietness was a clear indication that something was weighing heavily on her mind. She had been this way ever since we got back from the trip.

"Gee, you know you can talk to me about whatever is bothering you."

She said, "I know, but it's just so much that I wanted to forget that has happened in my past, and going back, revisiting the old neighborhood, even seeing my old friend CJ just made me think of things that I thought I had buried a long time ago."

"Things like what?" I asked.

"Well, I remember when we lived in Washington Height, my mother had a boyfriend. They eventually got married, but he was a horrible man."

"In what way?" I asked.

"He didn't seem too like me at all, and I'm not sure why. He seemed to like my older sister Valerie, but his dislike for me was very blatant. I know my mother had to have known how he felt, but she never said or did anything about it."

Then she went silent, seemingly lost in thought again. I didn't know if I should ask her to continue or just wait until she was ready to talk again. I felt that whatever it was, it must have been eating at her, and this wasn't the time to be pushy. We both sipped our coffee in silence.

Finally, she said, "Girl, you just don't know."

Well, I really didn't, but I was willing to listen and let her get it out of her system. I could clearly sense that whatever it was, it was going to be a very sensitive matter.

So I said, "Gee, sometimes talking about something helps us to heal and move on, especially with pain that we have buried so deep that we thought we had forgotten it or no longer felt it."

She said, "Yeah, I know, but this was something that I haven't thought about in years. I can't believe I'm thinking about it now."

"Well, if you want to talk about it, I'm here to listen, but I only want you to talk about it if you are ready."

I didn't want her to feel pressured, but at the same time I wanted her know that if she needed to release something that she had hidden for years, even from herself, maybe talking about it would help her to face it, accept it, and move on.

She cleared her throat and began to speak again.

She said, "That boyfriend I told you about was a very abusive man. I never understood why he didn't like me, but I never understood why my mother didn't stand up for me either."

"Do you think she might have been afraid of him?"

"I don't know, but she didn't seem to be, but I was so young that I really don't know. All I know is every Friday, they used to go partying and get drunk, come home, and that's mostly when the abuse would start. He never asked my older sister to do anything—it was always me. He wanted me to cook something for him and Momma to eat even though I was too young to be trying to cook. So usually, I'd make a sandwich or something and bring it to them, and if it was something that he didn't want, he'd start yelling and hitting me. Most of the time, he'd be so drunk that I could avoid him, but there were times when he did get a lick or two in."

Again I didn't know what to say, but I couldn't imagine living like that, but most of all, what mother would allow a man to strike her child and not say or do something? I think I finally began to understand her dislike for her mother.

"He was just so ugly during those times. He must have hated me, but I never understood why. Then about a year later, he and Momma decided to get married. I didn't know at the time, but she had gotten pregnant. It was a wedding that I never forgot because I wasn't allowed to attend. Now can you imagine a mother getting married and her daughter couldn't be there?"

No, I couldn't, but I didn't know what to say to that. I took that moment to get up and make us a fresh pot of coffee because this seemed like it was going to take some time to get through. This was going to be one of those times when you just rolled up your sleeves, sat back, and got ready for a long journey ahead. Gee didn't move; she sat in the chair seemingly lost in her own thoughts. She had a faraway look in her eyes, and I could tell she was reliving her past. A mother is supposed to protect her child at all cost, but after meeting Gee's mother, I knew that would not be the case with Pattie. I came in and sat down with two fresh cups of coffee; the aroma filled the room, and that put a smile on Gee's face, something I hadn't seen during this conversation.

As soon as I sat down, she started talking again.

She said, "I remember once after Momma got married, she and her husband came in so drunk they could barely stand, let alone walk. I don't see how they were able to drive home, but they did."

She went quiet again. I could tell she wasn't through talking but just needed to take a break before moving on to what she was about to tell me.

Then she said, "I knew I had to somehow escape before things got ugly again. We lived on the third floor of the apartment building, and the only thing I could think of was to jump out of the window because I knew if I didn't get away from those two that night, I was going to get a beaten. Ruth, girl, I just couldn't take anymore. So I eased up the window and jumped. At that moment, I didn't really care what would happen to me—all I knew I had to escape. So I jumped. Later, I woke up in the hospital. I don't remember much about the fall. When I opened my eyes, the doctor was leaning over me with a little flashlight looking into my eyes."

My own eyes filled with tears as I sat there listening to her story. It was almost like going back in time, being a child again and seeing everything through a child's eye. I had no words to express the feeling that I had inside me. I felt sad for my friend for having to go through such a hard time in her life at such a young age. I just held her hand, and I think my silence told her how I felt and what I was thinking. Now for sure I finally understood her feelings she had for her mother.

Then she said, "I overheard the doctor telling Momma that I was going to be all right, but they needed to keep me overnight for observation because I had a head injury, and they wanted to watch me to see if there was any more damage."

"Momma said, 'Doctor, could we speak to you a moment?'"

"Yes, sure," he said.

"I think we need to put my daughter in an institution because she's been acting strange lately. Maybe she needs psychological treatment. She's a handful, and this last act of hers proves she needs some kind of help. I'm at my wits' end and just don't know what to do anymore."

Gee said she couldn't believe her ears to hear her own mother trying to have her locked up in some kind of institution just to get rid of her. She said she was devastated, and because she was underage, she knew she wouldn't have any say-so in the matter. I thought, *How traumatizing that must have been for a child.* I couldn't imagine having to live through something like that and listening to your own mother having you put away and all for a man.

"The three of them went over to a corner of the room to discuss what my mother had told the doctor, but I overheard everything they were saying," she said. "I heard the doctor tell my mother that he needed to speak to one of the nurses on staff and that he would be right back because before anything could be done, there was paperwork that needed to be filled out. I just lay in that hospital bed wondering what I was going to do. I knew my mother had the upper hand. I was worried and wondering what was going to happen to me now. She said she knew her fate was in the hands of her mother and stepfather, and there was no one at that moment that she could think of to help her. She was only thirteen years old at the time and had no say-so in the matter. She said she never felt so alone and fearful at the same time. She said she lay there with tears in her eyes and a lot of mixed emotions, wondering.

She went quiet again, and I could sense that she was reliving that horrible time in her life. Although she was sitting right next to me, her mind had gone back years to that dark period. I sat quietly as well, not wanting to disturb her thoughts. She needed to relive that time in order to be able to talk about it, and hopefully, in the end, she could release the pain of her past and not let it interfere in her adult life. I got up to stretch my legs and give us both a break from talking.

After our short break, Gee continued with her story. "This time, I knew I was in trouble," she said. Listening to her mother, her stepfather, and the doctor discussing what to do next was very frightening for her. Her mother glanced back at her and figured out she was listening to the conversation, so she asked the doctor if they could talk outside in the hallway. Gee could no longer hear or make out what they were saying, only voices whispering. Sometimes their tones got loud, but mostly, they talked quietly. She knew at the moment her fate lay in their hands, and there was nothing she could do but abide by whatever decision they made.

Moments later, the three walked back in to tell her what had been decided. She said her hands were wet with sweat, and her heart was beating so loud she wondered if they could hear it. At last the doctor said she would be referred to a ward for observation, and then it would be decided where she would go from there, depending on the report the doctor got from the person who would do the observation. She just knew from the tone of his voice it wasn't going to be good, and looking into her stepfather's face, she knew he had a lot to do with what was happening to her. He seemed (to her) happier than she had ever seen him; she wasn't sure if it was happiness or relief, but either way, she knew he had made sure she wouldn't be returning to her home with them. His look told her everything she needed to know. She said at that moment, she felt so much hatred for her mother that she thought she would vomit. It was really hard for her to believe her own mother would allow her new husband to prompt her to make such a devastating decision.

She was in the hospital a week before the final decision was made. During that week, she wasn't allowed any visitors, not even her mother. She didn't really care whether she saw her or not because she was the reason she was there. She said she never felt so alone, and she cried herself to sleep every night. She finally said, "'If only I could see my sister Valerie,' I thought. Maybe she could've convinced Momma to let me come home."

I was thinking, *What an ordeal for a young child to go through alone.* She said that was the hardest week of her life, and she didn't understand how her own mother could do this to her. She spent a lot of time wondering how her mother could just desert her. She knew her stepfather didn't like her, but she didn't know her mother didn't like her either. She so wanted to see her sister Valerie and tell her what had happened to her, but she wasn't sure if she knew or not and even if she did, what could she do because she wasn't allowed to come see her.

Every morning, she was served breakfast. When lunchtime came, she was served lunch, and dinnertime, she was served dinner, usually by different kitchen staff. They never seemed friendly nor did any of them try to make conversation with her. They just spoke to her while setting up her tray. They always said, "Have a nice day and enjoy your meal" as they left the room. A nurse came in twice a day to check her vitals, ask how she was doing, and out they went. She didn't see the doctor at all during that week. There was no phone in her room, just a television. She said it was very lonely in that room with just a TV for company. She said she sometimes heard voices outside her room, or she would see someone walk by through the little window in the door. I really couldn't imagine what that was like because probably when I was thirteen, I would have been outside playing, running around with my friends.

At the end of the week, it had been decided that she would be placed in another ward, a suicidal trauma ward where she would be watched at all times. She said the routine there was just about the same as it was in the hospital. She was served three meals a day; the only other difference was different nurses came in three times a day. They always had a pad, taking notes as they spoke with her, and asked questions. She said her only question was wondering how long would she be there. She dared not ask for fear it would somehow get back to her mother, and that somehow might prolong her stay. As it was, she had no idea how long she would be there. No one had given her any indication as to how long her stay would be. She said she felt her mother was under some kind of spell with her new husband, and if he got wind of what she was asking, he might influence her to let Gee stay longer than necessary. She said she didn't know if her sister Valerie knew she was there, and even if she did, would she be allowed to come see her. She thought, *Somehow I have to get in touch with Valerie and let her know. Maybe she can come up with a plan to help her get out of there.* Even if they did have a plan of escape, where would she go? And how would she get out without someone seeing them?

I have to admit this was a lot even for me to take in. I just couldn't imagine how anyone could allow their child to be taken away and put in a psych ward at the age of thirteen. I believe something that dramatic would have to have an everlasting effect on a child. Gee went quiet again. I took that moment to get a break. I said, "Gee, let's take a walk and get some fresh air. Would you like that?"

She said, "Yes, let's do that. It's a beautiful sunny day outside, and some fresh air is just what we need."

Chapter 10

We took a long much-needed walk and ended up at a little ice cream shop with a few tables outside. We ordered some ice cream and sat outside, taking in the sun and watching people go in and out with their ice cream. Some mothers had little ones, and we could hear them saying in their tiny little voices, "I want vanilla" or another one saying, "I want chocolate." Sometimes, we'd hear a mother say, "Why not both?" with a laugh. The little voices made us both smile and think about our own grandchildren. If they were with us, they would probably be saying the same thing. It was a great distraction, and it really was a pleasant day to be outside. We took our time licking our ice cream cones while basking in the sun. We also took our time strolling back to Gee's house, talking about more pleasant things, the scenery around us, the colorful wildflowers, and the houses with the beautiful landscaped yards. We also talked about how we needed to get going on our plans to return to our home. The United States is such a massive place, so much to see and do and not feel cramped, making it hard to go back to our little cramped space in Bermuda.

Once we got back to her house, she wanted to talk some more, and I felt compelled to listen. She continued with her story. She said her Aunt Mattie had found out what had happened to her and came to see her at the hospital. She said her face lit up when her aunt walked in. She hugged her over and over and kept repeating how sorry she was that this had happened to her. She said she couldn't help wondering how did she find out, so she asked, "Aunt Mattie, how did you find out?"

Mattie replied, "I was in the grocery store the other day and saw your mom there. We talked for a while about small stuff, and finally, she said she had to put you away because you had been acting up. I asked, 'Put her away—what do you mean, put her away?' Momma told her what had happened and why I was in the hospital." Her aunt was appalled at what was going on so much so she insisted that Pattie tell her the whole story. Gee said after her mother had told her everything, her aunt came to the hospital and insisted on seeing her. She said she didn't know how, but somehow, she was allowed in to see her, and she had never felt so happy to see someone she knew. She said she and her aunt talked about the incident that led up to her being in the hospital.

Gee said, "In the middle of the conversation, Aunt Mattie got up and told me, 'Honey, I'll be right back. Hang in there,' and out the door she went. Girl, it's hard to explain how elated I felt that my aunt was there, and I just knew she was going to try to get me out of that horrible place. When she returned, the next thing I knew I was being released." Gee said that was best news she had heard in a long time. "But the absolute best news was, I wouldn't be going home to Momma and that monster. I was going to live with my Aunt Mattie and Uncle Pedro." One could hear the relief in her voice. There was paperwork to be filled out; she didn't care because at long last she would be leaving that awful, dreaded place that she had come to detest. She said she was overjoyed to know that she was going to live with her aunt and uncle in their home. Their children were all grown and had moved out. "Ruth, girl, that was the best news ever."

Once she got settled in with her aunt, she was able to see her sister Valerie and have fond visits with her. They had lots to catch up on during her absence. She said she knew her mother wasn't happy with the arrangement, and she was especially unhappy with how she felt her sister went behind her back and talked the doctor into allowing her take her away from the hospital without her permission. Gee said she didn't care what her mother thought; she was out, and that's all that mattered to her. She said she also knew that wouldn't be the end of it; her mother was bound to stir up some kind of trouble. She just wasn't the type to leave well enough along. The twins never did get along, and this incident just added more fuel to the fire.

Gee said she started to relax a little, but she knew something was brewing because she sometimes heard her aunt and her mother on the phone arguing, and from the sound of her aunt's voice, it wasn't pleasant. She said she wondered, *Why can't my mother just leave me along and let me be happy with my aunt?* Her mother was always a troublemaker and kept things stirred up, and this was going to be no exception. She said every time the phone rang, she jumped thinking it would be her mother calling to tell her aunt that she was going back to that facility. She said it also made her nervous and live in fear because she never knew what trick her mother was going to pull that would somehow get her taken from her aunt's house. For whatever reason, her mother never came to visit, just called, and Gee said she felt relieved that she didn't have to see her for now. She thought maybe she was too busy enjoying life with her new husband to think about her. Little did Gee know she was pregnant, but no one in the family seemed to have known at that time because if they did, no one talked about a pregnancy.

Gee settled in with her aunt and uncle as she prepared for the school year ahead. Looks like she would be living with them for a while. Her sister Valerie visited often, and she got news from her about her mother and her new husband; that's how she found out that her mother was having a baby. She said when she first heard the news, she was shocked. Her mother having a baby was unbelievable. And having a baby with that monster was most disturbing. She said her first thought in amazement was, *Momma is too old to be having a baby!* She didn't know what to make of that, but she knew she had to carry on, and with the help of her aunt and uncle, she had to get better and make the best of the situation she was in. As she talked, I couldn't help but wonder how in the world a thirteen-year-old child deal with such trauma in her life when she could have been thinking of things that most kids her age would have been. She now was happy not to be around the two (her mother and stepfather) of them with a baby coming. She couldn't help but wonder how her mother felt about this turn of events in her life. She had always lived such a carefree life, now this. Gee said she smiled to herself, thinking she couldn't possibly be happy about being pregnant.

Gee did have something to look forward to, school. She would be attending a new school, and she was hoping no one there would have heard about her misfortune over the summer. Her aunt took her shopping for new school clothes, and that was most exciting to her.

As excited as she was about her new life and her new school, she still thought about seeing a face in the crowd that looked like hers. That thought gave her hope that by some miracle, someday she might find out who her real father was. By now, she knew the man she had grown up thinking was her father was not. That was another subject that was never talked about, and she didn't know how to approach it with her aunt. She said she just couldn't take the risk of upsetting anyone by asking questions. That was a subject that she tucked away, hoping that someday she would get the answers she was looking for. She had too many other things to look forward to. This wasn't the time to open up old wounds. Right now, all she had was her aunt and uncle, and she didn't want to cause any unnecessary problems by bringing up the past.

She had about two weeks before school started. During those two weeks, she had a lot of time to think back to what had happened to her and how it all had turned out. It was hard to believe that a little over a week and a half ago, she was lying in a hospital bed for the criminally insane, and now she was in her aunt's house with her own room and some beautiful clothes to wear to her new school. She finally had something to smile about. Still, the rejection from her mother was very painful, which always had a way of slipping through her mind even when she had happy thoughts. She kept those thoughts to herself. She was in a happy place now and didn't want to jeopardize nor complicate her life any more than it already was.

The week before school started seemed to be going by fast, and as the time approached; she was getting nervous yet happy. Finally, the big day came, her first day at her new school. She had arisen early that morning to get dressed in one of her new outfits. She took her time getting dressed because she wanted to look her best. She heard her aunt coming down the hall to her room, and as she neared the door, she heard her call out, "Girl, are you up? You don't want to be late on your first day."

She replied, "Yes, Aunt Mattie. I'm up and already dressed." The door opened, and in came Mattie. "You look nice and fresh. Just remember your manners, young lady," her aunt said.

"Yes, ma'am, I will," Gee replied.

It was time to go outside and wait for the bus. As she stood outside waiting, she looked back, and sure enough, her aunt was standing in the doorway watching her as she suspected with a smile on her face. Finally the bus arrived. The driver opened the door for her and waited until she was seated before taking off. Riding to her new school, she said she wondered if anyone would be there that she knew from her old neighborhood, and if so, would they have heard about what had happened to her? She had all sorts of thoughts going through her mind. As the bus approached her new school, she was thinking how big the school was. Her new school was much bigger than her old school in her old neighborhood.

The bell sounded, and she said she jumped as her heart start racing with excitement. Well, so far, so good; she didn't see anyone that she recognized. Walking down the hall with tons of other students, it would have been hard to recognize a face because it was so many of them before her. She walked through the crowd, looking for room 11, which was her homeroom class. Her teacher's name was Ms. Miles. Each door had the name of the teacher on it, so that made it easier to know which room she would be going in. Finally, she saw it. She stood outside the door a minute, staring at the number on it before entering. She opened the door and walked in; the classroom was already about half full. She walked toward the middle of room, found an empty seat, and sat down. About two minutes later, the classroom seemed to have filled up. Ms. Miles stood up and introduced herself and to welcome the students in. She said, "Good morning, class. My name is Ms. Miles, and I will be your homeroom teacher." Gee said she was so excited to finally be in school. She said she looked around but didn't see any familiar faces. But she also said she knew this didn't mean she wouldn't because this was just her first day. She said she kept thinking she surely was going to meet someone from her past.

Ms. Miles was talking, but Gee said she was in deep thought thinking about her situation and hoping no one would ever find out. Finally, she brought her mind back to the present. "Well, class, today you will stay with me for the full day, and we will go over the details of your schedule for the rest of the week." She was thinking she wouldn't have to see any more students today except for the ones in her class. Tomorrow would be different.

Gee was so excited about her first day of school until she could think of nothing else. On her bus ride home, she had a happy smile on her face as she stared out the window. She was completely unaware of the person sitting next to her. She was thinking how much she was going to enjoy her new life away from Momma, the train wreck. Living with her aunt was a whole lot less stressful than living at home, and she knew her aunt would have a delicious meal waiting for her when she got in. That was one thing the twins had in common; they both loved to cook and to see that the people they cooked for enjoyed the meal. As the bus driver approached her stop, she couldn't wait to get off the bus to tell Aunt Mattie all about her first day of school. Her aunt heard the bus coming, and she was standing on the porch, waiting for Gee to get off with a big smile on her face.

"Hi, sweetie, how was your first day of school?"

Her Aunt Mattie asked, "Did you meet your teachers?" She was full of questions. "Did you see anyone that you knew?"

Gee responded, "Aunt Mattie, that was one of the best days ever, and no, I didn't see anyone that I recognize. My teacher, Ms. Miles, was really nice, and she explained to us that we would be going over our schedule and meet the rest of our teachers later this week."

She said her aunt replied, "That's good to hear. I'm happy things seems to be working out for you." I'm sure given that her niece had been through so much in the last few months, she just wanted to see a smile on her face and hear joy in her voice. She was so young to have gone through such a traumatic experience.

"Well," said Mattie, "come on in and tell me all about it." They talked about school for more than an hour, and finally, Mattie asked, "Chile, aren't you hungry yet?" She laughed. "I made your favorite, French fries and cheeseburger with onions just the way you like it." That put even a bigger smile on Gee's face as she realized that she was hungrier than she thought. They both got up and walked into the kitchen where Mattie prepared her plate. "Go wash your hands and when you get back the food will be on the table." Gee said she felt like she floated into the bathroom, washed her hands, and came back to sit down and enjoy her meal. She still was thinking about her good fortune, so much so she was constantly trying to talk between mouthfuls. Her aunt just had to stare and laugh.

Finally, it was time to go to bed; tomorrow was another day. Hopefully, it would be just as exciting as the first day. Gee was thinking she had another new outfit to wear the second day as well. She thought, *I have enough clothes that I can wear something different for the whole week.*

Upon arriving to school, she was thinking again, *Would this be the day that she might see a familiar face?* No matter how happy she was, that thought was a constant in her mind. She was going down the hall to her first period class, and she passed a boy in the hallway that she thought she recognized. It was so many students in the hall until she couldn't be sure. She tried looking back, but his back was turned to her, and she couldn't see his face. She made a mental note of his shirt so if she sees him again she would know to look closer. If that was who she thought he was, then he would be one grade ahead of her. She decided right then that when lunchtime came, she would make sure she got to cafeteria first. She wanted to get there as fast as she could so she could get a seat close to the door to watch as the students came in. Hopefully, she would see him before he saw her because when she passed him in the hallway, he didn't look her way.

When the bell rang for lunchtime, she hurriedly went to the lunchroom. Her eyes were glued to the doorway of the cafeteria; her heart was racing as she waited impatiently for the boy she had seen in the hallway earlier that day to come in. Students continuously filed in but not the face she was looking for. Finally, she gave up and sat down to eat alone. She thought even if he was in the cafeteria, there were so many faces around until it would have made it hard to find him, then she said she thought maybe his lunchtime wasn't the same as hers.

She said, "I thought to myself, 'Then tomorrow is another day. I will do the same thing tomorrow and the day after if I have to until I am sure that was him.' The next day, when the bell rang for lunch, I walked as fast as I could to make sure I got a seat close to the door as possible to wait and watch." She smiled as she was telling me that story.

She said as soon as the bell rang for lunchtime, she made a beeline for the cafeteria. She watched students filing in but no CJ. Finally, she was about to give up when CJ came strolling through the doorway—with a young boy swag no doubt. That was definitely him all right, she thought. He always had that swag and that air of confidence about him. She was stunned and happy at the same time. She looked down at her plate so he wouldn't see her as he passed her table. She did not move because she didn't know how she was going to approach him. That day, she had to pretend she hadn't seen him. She then said, "I had to come up with a plan on how I was going to handle things when I could finally muster up the courage to talk to him." He looked just as she remembered him, full of energy and an abundance of confidence. That was the CJ she had encountered back in the old neighborhood. She said she was very happy that she finally saw a familiar face and one from her old life, but she was still getting used to her new surroundings and all that went with it. Most of all, she didn't want to disappoint her aunt.

On her way home that day, she thought, she had lots to share with her aunt. She still couldn't believe that she saw an old friend from her old neighborhood, a boy she used to play with. She wondered if there were any more kids attending the same school, but still, a part of her was hoping she wouldn't run into anyone else because she didn't want her secret to get out. Although she knew CJ from before, she felt confident that he wouldn't expose her even if he knew because they had always been close and told each other their secrets. She said, "I always had a crush on CJ, and I felt he had a crush on me as well, but we were too young to act on our crushes, so we just played together and enjoyed being around each other."

The bus ride home was no different than the day before. As the bus rounded the corner to where she lived, her aunt was standing on the porch waiting just like she had the previous day. Only this time, she had some exciting news to share with her. She hurried up the steps to tell her aunt about seeing CJ. "How was your day at school today?" asked Mattie.

"Aunt Mattie, you will never guess who I saw today," said Gee.

"Who?" replied Mattie.

"CJ, I couldn't believe it was him. I thought I saw him yesterday, but I wasn't sure but it was actually him," Gee said breathlessly.

"Oh my, did you talk to him?" asked Mattie.

"No, but I know it was him because I saw his face but kind of hid from him so he wouldn't see me," Gee said.

"Why child, why?" Mattie asked.

"Well, I thought I'd wait until I knew what to say and to build up my confidence as to how I will approach him. I was taken aback and just wasn't quite ready to reveal myself," Gee said.

"Well, that's good you saw a familiar face. Now you can have someone to spend time with whom you are comfortable with," her aunt said. They talked more about school and CJ, but it was soon time for dinner, something Gee had forgotten among thinking about her day. Soon after dinner, she went to her room to have her thoughts all to herself.

All the way to school the next day, she was thinking of ways to approach CJ and what she would say to him once they came face to face. Well, she didn't have to wait long because shortly after she got off the bus, she ran into him. He was just as surprised as she was the first time she saw him. "Gee, Gee, is that you?" asked CJ.

"Yes," said Gee shyly. They hugged and made small talk before heading to their classrooms. They walked down the hallway together for a while then separated as they went to different classes.

"Let's catch up at lunch," said CJ.

"Okay, see you then," Gee said. She was thrilled that she saw someone she knew from before but still hoped he had not heard what had happened to her over the summer. She was thinking maybe he and his family had moved from the old neighborhood as well because why else would he be at the new school? She entered her classroom and thought they had lots to catch up on, but for now, she had to concentrate on her school work until then.

Lunch time finally came, and she could see CJ standing at the door waiting for her. They went in together, got their lunch, found a table, and sat down to eat and talk. Gee said she couldn't even remember what they had for lunch; she was so excited to see him and talk about the old times they shared back in the old neighborhood. She found out that his family had moved nearby, and that's why he was at the same school she was. They talked about everything trying to catch up during that one-hour lunch. Well, she was thinking, he must not have heard about what had happened to her during the summer because he didn't bring it up. They talked about general stuff, school, what classes they each were taking and what teachers they had. It was a very happy day for Gee, and she said she must have smiled the whole day. Things finally were going well for her.

Sometimes, she said, she still had dark moments that crept through her thoughts, but she kept them at bay. She had too many good things happening to her to let those dark thoughts spoil them. She was attending a new school, and now she had an old friend at that school, but most of all, she was away from her mother and her new husband, and that was truly something to be thankful for. Deep down, no matter what, she still, in some ways, missed her mother and being in her familiar environment. Life was good, and on that note, she fell asleep.

Gee told me that she now had so much to look forward to, her new school, living with her aunt, and now reconnecting with an old friend. She said she finally found peace and happiness. CJ was one year ahead of her in school, so they didn't take classes together but would see each other during recess and lunch time. They had made an agreement that they would meet at the cafeteria for lunch every day. She said she so looked forward to those times. They talked nonstop, even with mouthfuls, trying to catch up on what had been going on since they had last seen each other. She said CJ told her that he and his family had moved and he hadn't seen anyone from their old neighborhood. She said she was thinking so far he had not mentioned what had happened to her over the summer, so her secret seemed to be relatively safe. She was happy for that because that was something she wasn't ready to talk about with anyone. She said she was kind of surprised that her mother hadn't mentioned it to someone, and it might have gotten back to CJ's parents. It just wasn't like her mother to keep a secret.

Gee said, "Well, she is pregnant and had a new husband, so that must be taking up all her time." She had no idea how far along her mother was in her pregnancy nor did she know when the baby was due. She had been thinking about those things but didn't want to interrupt her own newfound happiness dealing with her mother's issues. She thought sooner or later, someone would mention it, and then she would know what's going on. Her aunt hardly ever mentioned her twin, and when she did, it was just in a casual way that couldn't be avoided. The aunt and uncle didn't seem to talk to each much either as far as she could tell. Her uncle hardly said anything; he usually stayed to himself. She knew he had a drinking problem, but she rarely saw him because shortly after dinner, he escaped to his room to watch reruns on TV or went out someplace and left her and her aunt alone.

Her aunt always made the same comment: "Well, we know where your uncle is going." That was all she would say about him, and the two of them would go on talking about whatever it was they were talking about before he left.

As she got ready for bed that night, she couldn't keep the smile off her face. She had so much to look forward to now that she had reconnected with CJ. They had a lot to talk about. She said CJ was her first crush. She kept that secret from her aunt, and she certainly didn't want her mother to find out. The thoughts that ran through her head that night made her have a pleasant, peaceful sleep.

The next morning, when she woke up, it was hard to not smile as she made her way to the kitchen for breakfast. Her aunt noticed the way she looked and commented on it. "Chile, you look very happy this morning. Did something happen that I don't know about?" She answered no and proceeded to eat her breakfast. She wasn't ready to share her secret with anyone, not even her aunt.

Finally, she was on the bus on her way to school. She could hardly wait to get there because she knew CJ would be waiting for her. As the bus pulled up, there he was with a big smile on his face that matched the way she felt. They talked as he walked her to her classroom. They parted ways at her classroom door with promises to meet for lunch. Gee said she'd hadn't been that happy for a long time. A different school, reconnecting with CJ, staying with her aunt, things were really working out and she couldn't be happier. She said she was thinking to herself this was going to be a great year after all.

As the school year progressed, she knew she had to focus on her school work. She studied hard because she wanted her aunt and uncle to be proud of her, and she also wanted to show them how much she appreciated what they were doing for her. She didn't want to give them any reason for doubt. She began to help out more around the house doing certain chores. She wanted to earn her worth.

On weekends, her sister Valerie came to visit her and kept her up to date on what was happening with the family, especially her mom and her new husband. She had been so drawn into her new life until she hardly even thought about her mom anymore. They were sitting outside on the porch one day when Valerie casually mentioned that their mom had had the baby. Gee was a bit surprised but didn't say much. Valerie said it was a girl, and her name was Pat, short for Patricia. Again, she kept her thoughts to herself but made a mental note to ask her aunt about the new baby. She was sure she knew but didn't want to upset her by bringing it up.

As I listened to Gee, I couldn't help but think, *What a family*. I knew every family had something going on, but Gee's family seemed to have more going on than any family I knew. Nothing was traditional about them, just the opposite.

Gee said she wondered about her new sister but didn't dare ask questions. All she knew it was a girl and her name was Pat. She was curious about what she looked like and couldn't help but wonder about her, but at the same time, she had to pretend not to care for fear of some kind of retaliation from her mother. Life with her aunt was good, and she didn't want to do anything that would jeopardize that.

One day, she came home from school and her aunt wasn't out on the porch to meet her. She thought that was unusual because she was always out there waiting. She got off the bus and went into the house. The house was dark and quiet. She said she called out, but no one answered. Her aunt was nowhere to be seen. She said she then knocked on her uncle's door but got no answer there. She then began to wonder what was going on. She went into the kitchen, turned on the light, and there she found a note on the table from her aunt. The note read she and her uncle had to leave, but she would explain everything when they returned. Gee said that was so unlike her aunt. She said she began to feel scared and anxious at the same time. She thought something must have happened very bad for them to have left a note for her. She said she couldn't eat or do anything; she just paced the floor while waiting for them to return. She said she knew something terrible had to have happened but wondered, *What could it be?*

Finally, after what seemed like hours, she heard her aunt's car pull up in the driveway. She ran to the door and out onto the porch. As her aunt and uncle got out of the car, she could tell something was terribly wrong. They walked up the steps onto the porch with stoic faces. Her aunt put her arms around her, crying. In her thirteen-year-old voice, she asked, "Aunt Mattie, what's wrong?"

In a broken voice, Mattie said, "It's Jason, he's gone."

Gee said, "Gone, gone where, what do you mean he's gone?" She said she got this deep feeling in her chest knowingly and not wanting to hear what she was about to say next.

Mattie said, "He was sick."

"What was he sick from, Aunt Mattie? What are you talking about?"

Then Mattie told her, "Jason's body was found floating under the Amoskeag Bridge." Gee said she was dumbfound; she didn't know what to say. She said she had heard rumors that Jason had been heavily into drugs, but after he left home, she didn't keep up with his whereabouts or his lifestyle.

She said, "After he moved out, I just assumed he was doing okay because Aunt Mattie never mentioned his name around me." She, her aunt, and her uncle just formed a circle hugging each other, crying. She had never heard her aunt cry so hard. They just sat down and cried and cried. She heard her aunt mumble that she needed to pull herself together because she had to take care of the funeral arrangements.

Gee said while she had compassion for what they were going through, she couldn't help but wonder if this new turn of events was going to affect her life in any way. She had gotten comfortable in her new home and didn't want anything to change that. She couldn't imagine what her aunt and uncle were going through, but she knew enough not to bother them as they both sat together quietly with tears streaming down their faces.

After what seemed like hours, her aunt got up and called her sister Cida. She told her what had happened and asked her to let some of the other family members know. She said she had a lot of other details to take care of, and it would help her out if she could reach out to them.

She noticed that she didn't call her twin sister, Pattie. She said maybe she didn't call her because she had a new baby to take care of, but deep down inside, she knew that wasn't the reason; there had always been bad blood between those two, and she knew her mom probably wouldn't care one way or the other or she would say something nasty to further upset her aunt. As she was telling me the story, she said, "How pathetic, she couldn't share something so personal with her own twin sister. She had to call her older sister and share the news with her. I know Aunt Mattie didn't call Momma. It had to have been my Aunt Cida that called and told her the news. As a matter of fact, I don't remember Momma calling my aunt at all." Even then, she looked a little perplexed. I was just sitting there trying to imagine what had to be going through her mind with such overwhelming news. Like I said earlier, I had never met a family like Gee's family; they were characters unlike any I had ever encountered. As I got to know Gee's family through her, I had to agree her mother was more than little crazy. I would go as far as to say she was insane.

She said after the funeral, everything seemed to have gone back to normal—well, as normal as could be under the circumstances. She returned to school, and her aunt and uncle went back to their life as usual. She did say, "My aunt was a bit quieter. She still welcomed me home every day from school, but I could see that she wasn't as enthusiastic as she used to be." She said her uncle went back to drinking, only now it seemed like he was drinking more. She said she did notice that he seemed to becoming more and more distant. He was staying in his room more also. The only time she saw him was at dinnertime, and when he finished eating dinner, he escaped back to his room, and she wouldn't see him again until dinnertime the next day.

She said, "I noticed that he seemed to be getting frail. He was never a large man, but his physique seemed to be shrinking." She hesitated a moment before going on. "He didn't eat much. He ate very little, which made me wonder if he was sick and Aunt Mattie didn't want to tell me about it." She said in her thirteen-year-old mind, she had other things to worry about, school and now CJ. "Just thinking of him made me smile."

One day, she and her aunt were sitting out on the porch just relaxing and she asked, "Aunt Mattie, where is Uncle Pedro?"

She answered, "Chile, he's in his room drunk probably. He rarely comes out of his room anymore except to eat. I've tried to get him to come sit on the porch with me in the evenings, but he refused. He doesn't say much, and I just leave him alone, thinking he's still grieving about what happened to Jason."

Then as an afterthought, she said, "Ain't much I can do about that. I'm still having a hard time thinking about how we lost him myself." Gee said this time, Aunt Mattie seemed lost in her thoughts. Gee said she understood what had happened, but she wanted things to go back to the way they were before the tragedy.

Gee was allowed to stay with her aunt and uncle until she finished high school. When she graduated from high school, she went off to college and began to explore what college life was all about. She was an adult now and could make her own decisions. She no longer had to worry about her mother. She said she still kept up with family news through her sister Valerie.

Chapter 11

Things had been going well for Gee until she got a call from Valerie. She called to tell her their mother's husband had gotten killed in a car accident. "Really, when?" asked Gee.

Valerie gave her the details of the accident according to what her mother said. Gee asked, "How's Pat?" She was only eight years old at the time, but she was concerned about her. Although she wasn't close to her younger sister, she was still concerned about her. She said she had only seen her a few times, and that's when Valerie would sneak her over to her aunt's house for visits.

I asked Gee about her mother's husband. "I didn't attend their wedding, and I surely wasn't going to attend his funeral. Honestly, Ruth, I really didn't care what had happened to him. My only concern was for my younger sister. Girl, I can't tell you much because I never left school for any of what was going on. I was glad he was gone. In my mind, I was thinking he got what he deserved."

As an afterthought, she said, "I know that might sound horrible, but it's true. He probably was drunk. The way he and Momma used to drink, I'm surprised she wasn't in the car with him."

Valerie did tell her there weren't many people there on their mother's side of the family. Mattie and Cida weren't there and none of their children. "I think I saw Uncle Jimmy's son there, but I'm not sure. I only went because of Momma," Valerie told Gee. "I didn't know his family, so I supposed the few people that were there was his family."

Valerie did tell Gee their mother carried on something terrible. "You should have heard her. I thought at one point she was going to try to get in the casket with him," she said laughing. "It was hysterical." Gee said they had a good laugh about that, picturing their mother. Valerie said after the funeral, she felt compelled to drive her mother home and spend some time with her since she had no one else. Valerie told Gee as soon as they walked in the house, their mother went and poured herself a big glass of scotch and started in on her sisters, Mattie and Cida. "Can you believe neither one of those SOBs came to my husband's funeral?"

"Mattie of all people should have been there."

Gee said, "I can't imagine why." She said Valerie told her she stayed as long as she could stand to listen to their mother go on and on about what a good husband he was and how she was going to miss him. "My sister said after about two hours of Momma, she had to leave. I really don't see how she stayed that long. I didn't even call her at all."

After college, Gee met a man, got married, and moved to California. From that marriage, she had her daughter, Amber. The marriage didn't last, but she and her daughter stayed in California for quite a few years. She said putting distance between her and her family drama was good for her. She only heard about it from talking with her sister; she no longer had to live with it or become mixed up with whatever was going on with the family. She had finally found some peace.

Chapter 12

A FEW YEARS LATER VALERIE CALLED. THIS TIME, it was about her Uncle Pedro. He had died from a heart attack. Gee said she was in shock. Although she didn't want to go back to her hometown, she knew she had to for her aunt's sake. She said she kept thinking what would have happened to her if it hadn't been for them. So she packed for her and her daughter to make the trip. This would be her first trip back since leaving Jasper.

Valerie picked her and her daughter up from the airport. In the car on their way to her aunt's house, Valerie filled her in on the details of Pedro's death. She said their aunt was taking his death pretty hard.

Before all this happened, according to Gee, her mom had already disassociated herself from most of the family. What I gathered from my conversation with Gee, something was wrong with her mom's phone. It seemed when she tried calling someone, the call immediately went to the person's voice mail. Given the way her mom was, she just assumed that everyone had blocked her calls, and she took this personally. Little did anyone know how personally she had taken it.

Now her aunt had the task of making arrangements for her husband's funeral. Just a few years ago, she was making arrangements for their son's funeral. Her aunt had one daughter and one son, and they came to help their mom with the arrangements. She said she was happy to see her cousins because she hadn't seen them in years. She said the last thing she had heard about Turk, he was in rehab. She thought, *Well, it must have worked because he looks good.* Mattie's daughter, who had moved away right after college, rarely came home for visits anymore. By now, she had gotten married and started her own family.

Gee said, "I always thought she looked so sophisticated."

During the time before the funeral, Gee said she was in awe of the different people coming around, people she hadn't seen in years. The house seemed full most of time, people bringing food along with well-wishes or just to pay their condolences. Her aunt's house wasn't a big house, and it seemed smaller with all the people coming in and out. The kitchen was tiny, but it was cramped with all sorts of dishes full of food. She said it felt like they could have fed an army—literally. I smiled as she told that story because that's exactly how it was in the South. People didn't do much visiting, but when a family member died, everyone seemed to come around to show respect and not without a container of food.

The day of the funeral was horrible. There was one family friend, Ms. Turner, who had been a friend as far back as she could remember. She said Ms. Turner was happy to see her, and she hugged her tight. Then she said, "Look at you, all grown up and now living in California. I'm so happy for you. Mattie told me what happened to you that summer after your mother married that scum. I'm glad she and Pedro were able to take you in, child, because it was a shame your mother allowed that man to come into her life and change everything." She exchanged small talk with a few other people before making her way to her seat.

It was finally time for the family to march in. Gee said the small church was packed. She said she noticed her mother wasn't with the family, and she couldn't believe she wouldn't attend her own sister's husband's funeral. "But of course, Aunt Mattie didn't attend Momma's husband's funeral," Gee said.

They all marched in and took their seats, and then this big commotion broke out. She looked up her eyes wide in sheer horror. Lo and behold, there was her mother standing in front of the casket, hollering, "Lola, where the hell have been? I've been trying to call you forever, and you have blocked my number. You know my husband died, and you didn't come to his funeral. I can't believe you." Everyone was quiet, and my mother just wouldn't shut up; she kept going. "I know all of you have blocked my number because everyone I called, I get the same voice mail message. Now I want to know what the hell is going on with all of you." She just wouldn't sit down and shut up. Gee said she had her fist balled up like she was ready for a fight.

She looked at Ms. Turner and said, "Lola, you of all people just keep ignoring me. I can't believe you would treat me like this—we've been friends forever. Now you got the audacity to show up here! My own daughter came all the way from California to attend Pedro's funeral and wouldn't come when my husband died. I just can't believe you people."

Gee said her mother looked like someone that had lost their mind, with spit flying and eyes bulging out of her head. Then she said, "She didn't stop there—she actually tried to get to Ms. Turner with her arms raised ready for a fight until some men from the church got up to hold her back and take her outside. Gee said she had never been so embarrassed before in her life. When she was telling me that story, I had to laugh because I could only imagine what that incident must have looked like—like a scene from one of Tyler Perry's Madea movies. One thing for sure was I didn't have to think her mother was crazy or no longer wonder why she would say such a thing about her. I knew without a doubt, she was absolutely crazy.

She said after they took her mother outside, a couple of the men had to stand guard at the door so she wouldn't try to come back in. She said her mother could be heard inside the church screaming and hollering at Mattie with all kind of foul language. Then she screamed, "Mattie, you ain't no saint. Everybody knows about your secret."

"When she said that, you could hear the whole church grasp," Gee said. "Everyone was quiet as a mouse. I wished I could have disappeared. I felt so bad for my aunt." According to Gee, Pattie was ranting and raving so much, so the police had to be called to take her away. Gee said just before she was put into the police car, she heard her yell out, "I didn't like Pedro anyway, and I'm glad he's gone, ha ha!" She said she was hoping her aunt didn't hear that last statement, but with the way her mother was screaming, everyone had to have heard her.

Gee said after all that disruption, the funeral finally got on the way, but it was a day to remember. She said her mother had given the community something to talk about for a long time, and that wasn't hard to believe, but I could never have imagined such a commotion, especially at a funeral.

"Girl, I had to wonder if life would ever get back to the way it was." I could tell she was still having some deep thoughts about the incident. Then she said, "Ruth girl, I never thought we would ever get over that because nothing like that had ever happened that I know of."

I was thinking most people would have been grieving, not fighting; still, I couldn't help but smile to myself as I pictured the scene in my mind. I was picturing a crazed-looking lady all dressed up with a wild look in her eyes; hat probably was crooked on her head, ready to swing at anyone that got in her way with her purse in one hand and a balled fist attached to her other arm. What a scene that must have been.

Gee and I had lots of long talks about the goings-on in her family. From those talks, I finally figured out what the twins' secrets were without Gee having to tell me. After listening to all the stories from Gee and some of the things she told me, it wasn't that hard to figure out what those two knew about each other. Little did I know that there were ever more secrets in that family.

Gee's mother had a one-night stand, and she was the result of that. Also, it seemed that Mattie too had a one-night stand, and her only daughter was the result of that. Gee's mother wasn't married at the time of her one-night stand, but Mattie was. She was married to Pedro. They had to have known about each other's secrets but somehow kept it among themselves.

It turned out that her aunt even had a darker secret. She said her Aunt Cida knew about the twins' secrets but never talked about it as far as she knew. Gee said, "Rumor had it that Aunt Mattie's second son wasn't her husband Pedro's—it was his brother's child. When Jason found out the truth, he had a hard time dealing with the fact that the man who raised him wasn't his biological father—in fact, he was his uncle. But guess who told Jason? Momma." That wasn't hard to believe because Gee's mom was very vindictive and unpredictable.

The truth was too much for him to deal with. Gee said Jason started drinking heavily until one day, he just didn't come home. For days, no one had seen or heard from him. Then four days later, he was found floating in the water under a bridge. He didn't leave a note, but it was speculated that once he found out the truth about his identity, he just couldn't deal with it and jumped off the bridge. Gee said, "Aunt Mattie and Uncle Pedro took his death hard. I'm not sure if Uncle Pedro knew the truth or not, but I know Aunt Mattie did. I often wondered if Uncle Pedro knew the truth as well and if that was the reason for his drinking problem."

As an afterthought, Gee said, "I'm not sure if my cousin Tracy (Mattie's daughter) even knew. All I know is that once she got married, she rarely came for visits anymore." I could tell by the look on her face that she was in deep thought again. "I noticed Tracy was distant from the family because she never attended family gatherings nor did she come home for holidays. If it wasn't for the funeral, I don't think she would have come then."

I wished Gee could let go of all the baggage that she had carried around for years and find peace within herself. The she said, "You know, whenever someone asked Aunt Mattie about Tracy, she always gave the same answer, 'Well, you know how the young folks are. She has her own family now, and she's quite busy with the new baby and all.'"

Gee seemed lost in thought. "Girl, my family secrets are like still waters—they run deep. Now that I'm thinking about it, my family must have had a generational curse because according to Aunt Cida, their mother, my grandmother, got pregnant with the twins while she was married to someone else as well." She laughed as she said that. She shrugged.

"Aunt Cida also said they had a gay aunt. They didn't know she was gay at the time because one's sexuality wasn't something that was talked about. They knew she was different but didn't quite understand why." Aunt Cida told her that this aunt rarely came around the family, and when she did, she always brought her special friend with her. Gee said her aunt said they didn't think much of it because their aunt always said they were just roommates, but as time went on, they figured it out. "I think my Aunt Cida knew all the family secrets, but she kept them to herself."

Chapter 13

We returned to Bermuda, happy to get back to our everyday lives. Strangely, once we were home, Gee spoke very little of her family. She was her old self again, just as talkative as ever. It was almost like the week we spent with her family hadn't happened. I didn't bring up her family drama for fear of stirring up old memories. I didn't want her mood to change. I wanted to ask her how she was doing after that visit, but it was as if her mind had blocked out all the pain of the past. We resumed our beloved outings, going to the beach to people-watch and just hanging out together on weekends cooking our favorite meals, inviting a few people we knew over every now and again for an outdoor barbecue. Everything was back to normal, and I must say I was glad to be home and away from the drama that seemed to have plagued Gee's family throughout the years. I thought, *That kind of drama is toxic*, and the sooner I got away from it, the better I'd feel. I had hoped that would be the last time I'd see those people.

I remember when we left Gee's mother's house, she said I was welcome to come back anytime. She said, "Ruth, you and your husband will be more than welcome to come for visit. I'd love to have you guys." I also remember thinking to myself that she wouldn't have to worry about me coming back because one visit with her was enough to last a lifetime. Of course, at that time, I was gracious enough to thank her, knowing I had no intentions of coming back.

About a year later, I received a call in the middle of the night. I bolted up, fearing the worst. Late-night calls usually aren't good. "Hello?" I whispered, trying not to wake up my husband.

Then I heard Gee's voice. "Ruth, I'm sorry to have to call so late, but I just got a call that my Aunt Mattie is in the hospital—she has had a heart attack."

"Oh, Gee, I'm so sorry to hear that. How is she?"

"I talked with Valerie, and she said she's hanging in there but I should come as soon as I can," she said.

I asked, "Well, what can I do to help?"

Gee said, "As you know, this is a busy time for my husband. Tourist season is just starting, and he won't be able to get off work, so I was hoping you could go with me."

I said, "Sure, you make the arrangements and call me with the details."

Gee said, "Thanks, Ruth. I don't know what I would do without you."

I said, "Now go back to bed and try to get some rest. Tomorrow, you can get everything done."

We hung up the phone, but I couldn't get back to sleep. I had to think and wait until morning to talk to my husband. He's a heavy sleeper, so he never woke up. I, on the other hand, tossed and turn in between sleeping. It was a restless night because I felt very fatigued the next morning. I was also thinking what I needed to do to prepare for the trip. Thankfully, I had done the laundry the day before. Usually when I take trips, I always prepare meals for my husband in advance, but this time, there was no time to take care of that detail; he'd have to be on his own.

The next morning, Gee called to give me the details of our trip. She said, "I've made all the necessary arrangements. We will fly out tomorrow on the ten twenty flight if that's okay with you."

"Sure, I'll start packing now. Do you know how long we will be staying?"

"I'm not sure. I just booked one-way tickets."

"Okay, see you tomorrow morning."

The next morning, we rushed to the airport, barely making our flight. We flew to Atlanta, where we had a connecting flight to Jasper, Missouri. As we sat in the boarding area waiting for our connection, Gee decided to call her mom. She said she was going to put her on speaker so I could hear the conversation. She turned the volume down, hoping the other passengers wouldn't hear the conversation, and dialed the number.

"Good morning, Momma. How's Aunt Mattie?" Then she went on to say, "Ruth and I are in Atlanta waiting for our flight to Jasper."

"What! You are on your way here?" Pattie replied coldly.

"Yes, Momma, I'm on my way there. I should be there around two thirty today."

Gee took a deep breath and rolled her eyes up at the ceiling while shaking her head. She leaned over and whispered to me, "Girl, I knew this wasn't going to go well."

Then Gee asked, "Momma, have you been to the hospital to see your sister?"

"No, I haven't, and I'm not going, so don't try to lay a guilt trip on me," Pattie replied. "What good is my sitting in some germ-infested hospital room going to do? It's not going to change anything. If it's your time to go, then it's your time." With that comment, Pattie hung up the phone.

Gee was stunned, and so was I. We just looked at each other, bewildered. If it wasn't such a serious situation, it would have been comical. I was thinking to myself, *Gee's mom is more than a trip—she's a journey.*

I wanted to do something special for Gee to, so I got up and went to the ticket agent to see if we could get upgraded seats, thinking that might help Gee and put her in a better mood. I explained our situation to the ticket agent and asked if we could be upgraded. She was very sympathetic. She looked at her screen and said, "Sure, looks like we have a few seats left in first class." She gave us two first-class seats for a fifty-dollar fee each. I paid the fee without telling Gee what I had done. I was hoping this little surprise would perk her up; even if it was a short flight, it would be a comfortable one. Once we boarded the plane, she was quite surprised where we were seated. Although it was 1 o'clock in the afternoon, I had the complimentary glass of wine, and so did Gee. We toasted each other with a smile.

When we arrived in Jasper, we went straight to the hospital. Some of Gee's family was already there: her Aunt Cida, her cousins, Sonny and Mattie's daughter, Tracy. After hugs and hellos, Gee was allowed to go in for a few minutes to see her Aunt Mattie. She was still in ICU, but the hospital staff gave her permission to have a short visit with her. I sat with the family, giving Gee some alone time with her aunt. Sonny said she was still awake, and she seemed stronger today than she did yesterday. When Gee's visit was over, she and I went with Tracy to her aunt's house where we would be staying. It had been a hectic day, and I was glad to have someplace to lie down and rest. We had plans to meet Gee's sister Valerie at the hospital the next morning for the eight thirty visitation. I was exhausted, but I knew I wasn't going to get much sleep. This family had a way to wear a person out without even trying.

As I was getting ready for bed, Gee peeked her head in the door and said, "Good night. Love you, my friend."

I said, "Love you back," giving her a smile. With that, she closed the door, and hopefully, she went to bed.

Morning came fast. Seems like I had just fallen asleep when I heard a knock on the door telling me it was time to get up. I dragged myself out of bed, got dressed, and we were on our way to hospital. I was hoping to grab a cup of coffee on the way, but Tracy didn't stop. Gee looked back at me and said, "Girl, we can get some coffee from the hospital cafeteria."

Wow! I thought. She must have read my mind. I gave her a nod with a smile. Valerie was already there when we arrived. Thankfully, she had brought some blueberry scones, which were perfect with the hot coffee.

Gee asked Valerie, "Have you talked to Momma yet?"

Valerie replied, rolling her eyes, "Yes, but you can imagine how that went. I called her last night to give her an update on Aunt Mattie's condition, and she didn't want to hear about it."

Gee said, "I know, right?"

Then Valerie went on to say, "I had been at the hospital for hours waiting to see her before going home. I must have just missed you guys by an hour because Sonny called and told me you had just made it."

Gee then told her about the conversation she'd had with their mother. "I called her from the airport to let her know I was coming, and she had nothing but ugly things to say. When she finished spewing out trash, she hung up in my face. Just like our mom, huh?"

Valerie agreed wholeheartedly with her sister.

A few minutes later, a nurse came out to tell Gee, Valerie, and Tracy they could go in and see Mattie. The nurse said, "Don't stay too long. We don't want her to be too tired when the doctor comes around to check her." They agreed they wouldn't stay just wanted her to know they were there. "We really only allow two people in at a time, but I understand that you traveled a long way to see your aunt, so I'm going to make an exception this time. Enjoy your visit." With that comment, she left them alone for their visit. When the doctor came to examine Mattie, the ladies came out. When he finished with the examination, he came to give them a report. He said they were able to do a cardiac angioplasty and put in a stent. She seemed to have responded well to the treatment. Then the doctor told them they were going to keep her in ICU for another day before transferring her to a room.

Once the doctor left, Gee and I went in to see her. She looked weak but alert. Her eyelids appeared heavy, no doubt from the medications. She was in good spirits, and that was a good sign. We didn't stay too long, but I noticed that she never asked about her twin.

Gee and I returned to the waiting room to allow Tracy some private time to spend with her mother. We sat there watching old episodes of the *Golden Girls*. Finally, Tracy came out and sat with us. In the midst of what was going on, Gee forgot that I had never met Tracy. Then she said, "Tracy, I forgot to introduce you to my friend Ruth."

I extended my hand and said, "Hello, Tracy, it's good to meet you, just wish it had been under different circumstance."

She said, "So do I, but it's good to meet you as well. I've heard so much about you I feel as if I know you already. We drove home to my mother's house without thinking about introductions and to the hospital this morning."

Gee said, "I know, what was I thinking?"

I responded, "Everyone was so preoccupied I didn't take it personally—I totally understand." All three of us just laughed; it kind of felt good to have something to laugh about.

The three of us sat in the waiting room, waiting to get an update report on Mattie. When the doctor came out, he stated that she was doing well, much better than expected, and she would be put in a room as soon as one became available. I thought that was good news, which meant Gee and I wouldn't have to spend that much time in Jasper; we could go back home in a reasonable time.

We did stay long enough to make sure her Aunt Mattie was going to be all right. Gee didn't visit with any of the other family members, only her sister Valerie. Once Mattie was released from the hospital, her daughter Tracy took her home and promised to stay with her until she was completely on her feet. Mattie was a strong woman; she had survived a lot and soon got back to her old life.

I knew this family was different; I could sense that from the first time meeting them. They were characters you read about, not the kind you would want to live among.

About the Author

Martha Wyatt-Rossignol was raised in a small town in Mississippi. She now resides in Manchester, New Hampshire. She's the youngest of six children born to Shelby Davis Wyatt and Verine Sanders Wyatt. Martha attended school in Jefferson County where she excelled in her classes. She graduated high school in 1968, being among the first of a few to integrate the heavily segregated school system.

Shortly after high school, Martha married her longtime boyfriend, and they had two beautiful daughters, Nichole Renee and Teresa LaShea Rossignol. After her first marriage ended in divorce, she met her second husband, Joseph Rossignol, while working at a local supermarket in Fayette, Mississippi.

Martha is a real-life socialite. She has traveled to places near and far. She's also lived in California, Nevada, Georgia, and Bermuda; but she made New Hampshire her home. When she's not traveling, she enjoys spending time with family and friends, especially her great-grandchildren, Chauncy and Aubrey, and her grandson Tommy. She's truly the life of the party! She especially loves spending time at her "happy place"—her home—where she regularly exercises her talents, interior decorating.

Martha has also previously published a book, "*My Triumph over Prejudice: A Memoir*".